Banana Cookbook for Beginners

Discover a New World of Flavors with Over 200 Easy, Delicious and No-Fuss Homemade Banana Recipes to Get Healthy and Feel Great!

Joanna Greace

Table of Contents

Bananas contain a specific protein (tumor necrosis factor) that helps prevent oncological conditions. Ripe fruits have much more of it in them, so **it's recommended to eat bananas with spotted or darkened skin.**

Mineral deficiency is a common cause of ankle muscle spasms. By consuming products as rich in potassium and magnesium as bananas, **you can prevent muscle cramps**. That's why many athletes include them in their diet

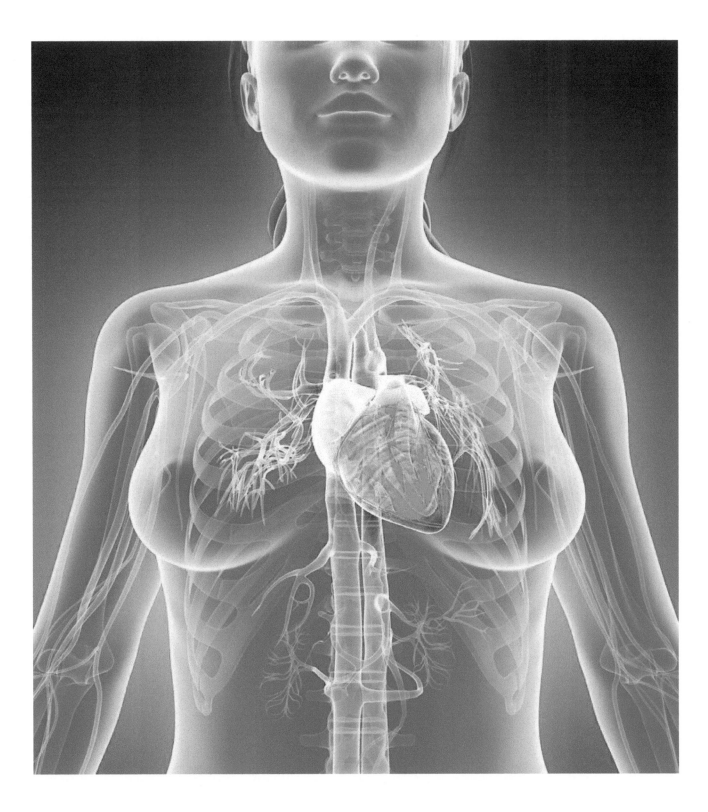

A potassium-rich diet is recommended to those who have high blood pressure and are prone to cardiovascular diseases. Daily consumption of 1.3 grams of this element **decreases the risk of cardiac events by 26%**. To supply that amount to your body, you should eat 2 to 3 bananas a day, depending on their weight

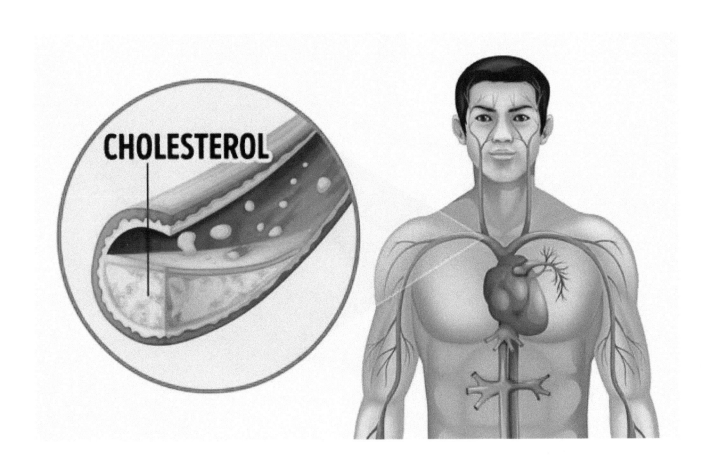

Cholesterol is the main cause of vascular obstruction, which leads to atherosclerosis. Bananas contain phytosterols that help reduce the levels of cholesterol in your blood and **maintain your vascular system's health**

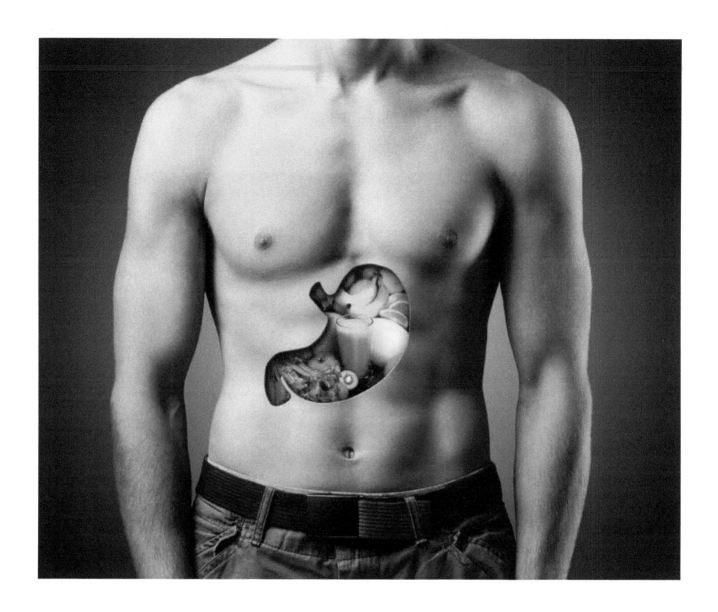

Bananas are recommended to people with gastric ulcers and those who're in the risk group. They contain a special enzyme that increases the secretion of mucus that protects the abdominal walls

The abundance of vitamins and minerals make bananas a great source of energy. Simple carbs are quick to digest and can replenish your energy resource almost immediately if need be

Moist Banana Raisin Bread

Ingredients

1 1/2 tablespoons butter, melted
1/3 cup white sugar
1/3 cup peanut butter
1 egg, lightly beaten
1 ripe banana, mashed
1 1/2 tablespoons milk
1 cup all-purpose flour
1/2 teaspoon baking powder
1/4 teaspoon baking soda
1 dash salt
1/2 cup raisins
1/4 cup chopped roasted peanuts

Directions

Preheat oven to 350 degrees F (175 degrees C). Grease a 5x9 inch loaf pan.

In a large bowl, cream together the butter, sugar, peanut butter, egg, banana, and milk. In a separate bowl, mix the flour, baking powder, baking soda, and salt. Stir the flour mixture into the butter mixture just until moistened. Fold in the raisins and peanuts.
Transfer to the prepared pan.

Bake 45 minutes in the preheated oven, or until a knife inserted in the center of the loaf comes out clean. Cool in pan for 10 minutes before serving.

Granny's Banana Bread

Ingredients

2 1/4 cups all-purpose flour
1 teaspoon baking soda
1/2 teaspoon ground cinnamon
1/2 teaspoon ground nutmeg
1 cup white sugar
2 eggs
1/3 cup unsweetened applesauce
4 ripe bananas, mashed
1 tablespoon vanilla extract
1 cup raisins (optional)
1 cup chopped walnuts (optional)

Directions

Preheat oven to 375 degrees F (190 degrees C). Lightly grease and flour a 9x5 inch loaf pan.

In a large bowl, stir together flour, baking soda, cinnamon, nutmeg and white sugar. Stir in eggs, applesauce, bananas and vanilla extract. Fold in raisins and nuts if desired. Pour batter into prepared pan.

Bake in preheated oven for 45 to 60 minutes, until a knife inserted into center of the loaf comes out clean.

Chocolate Banana Martini

Ingredients

1 teaspoon chocolate syrup
1 (1.5 fluid ounce) jigger banana liqueur
1 (1.5 fluid ounce) jigger coffee flavored liqueur
1/3 cup milk
1 cup crushed ice
1/2 banana, peeled and sliced lengthwise into quarters

Directions

Drizzle chocolate syrup round the inside of a martini glass.

Combine banana liqueur, coffee liqueur, milk, and ice in a shaker. Shake vigorously, and strain into martini glass. Garnish with banana spears.

3

Ingredients

1 (18.25 ounce) package yellow cake mix
1 (3.5 ounce) package instant banana pudding mix
4 eggs
1 1/2 cups milk
1 1/2 cups white sugar
1/4 cup all-purpose flour
3/4 cup butter
3/4 cup shortening
3/4 cup milk
1 1/2 teaspoons banana extract

Directions

Preheat oven to 350 degrees F (175 degrees C). Grease and flour 2 - 9x13 inch pans.

In a large bowl, stir together the cake mix and instant pudding. Beat in the eggs and 1 1/2 cup of milk. Divide the batter evenly between the two pans.

Bake in preheated oven for 15 to 17 minutes, or until a wooden toothpick inserted into the cake comes out clean. While the cake is baking, make the filling.

Stir together the sugar and flour. In a medium bowl, cream together the butter, shortening and sugar mixture. Beat in the milk and banana extract until smooth.

When the cake is cooled, invert onto a serving tray. Spread filling over the top and cover with remaining layer of cake. Keep chilled until 1/2 hour before serving.

Ingredients

1 (18.25 ounce) package yellow cake mix
2 (3.5 ounce) packages instant vanilla pudding mix
1 (8 ounce) package cream cheese
1 1/2 cups milk
3 ripe bananas
2 (8 ounce) cans crushed pineapple, drained
1 (16 ounce) package frozen whipped topping, thawed
1 (4 ounce) jar maraschino cherries, drained
1/4 cup chopped walnuts

Directions

Bake cake as directed on package. Cool completely.

In a medium bowl, combine pudding, cream cheese and milk. Beat until smooth. Spread on cake.

Slice bananas thin and arrange on top of pudding mixture. Spread drained pineapple on top of bananas.

Cover entire cake with whipped topping. Garnish with cherries and chopped walnuts.

Banana Loaf Cake I

Ingredients

1 1/2 cups all-purpose flour
1 cup white sugar
1/4 cup butter, softened
1 teaspoon vanilla extract
1 teaspoon baking soda
1/2 teaspoon baking powder
1 egg
3 very ripe bananas

Directions

Preheat oven to 350 degrees F (175 degrees C). Grease and flour a 5x9 inch loaf pan

Mash bananas and add flour, sugar, butter, vanilla, baking powder, baking soda and egg. Mix well. Pour into loaf pan.

Bake at 350 degrees F (175 degrees C) for 50 to 60 minutes, or until toothpick inserted into center of cake comes out clean.

Banana Streusel Pie

Ingredients

1 (9 inch) unbaked pastry shell
1/4 cup sugar
1/2 teaspoon ground cinnamon
1 teaspoon cornstarch
1/2 cup pineapple juice
2 tablespoons lemon juice
1 1/2 teaspoons grated lemon peel
4 cups sliced ripe bananas
STREUSEL:
1/2 cup all-purpose flour
1/2 cup packed brown sugar
1/3 cup chopped macadamia nuts or almonds
1 teaspoon ground cinnamon
1/4 cup butter or margarine

Directions

Line the unpricked pastry shell with a double thickness of foil. Bake at 450 degrees F for 10 minutes. Remove the foil and bake 2 minutes more or until pastry is golden brown; set aside. Reduce heat to 375 degrees F.

In a saucepan, combine the sugar, cinnamon and cornstarch. Add the pineapple juice, lemon juice and peel; mix well. Cook and stir until thickened and bubbly; cook and stir 2 minutes more. Remove from the heat. Fold in bananas; pour into crust.

For streusel, combine flour, brown sugar, nuts and cinnamon; cut in butter until the mixture resembles coarse crumbs. Sprinkle over the filling. Cover edges of pie with foil. Bake at 375 degrees F for 40 minutes or until topping is golden and filling is bubbly. Cool on a wire rack.

Icy Banana Milkshake

Ingredients

2 bananas, peeled and sliced
6 ice cubes
5 cups milk
1/2 cup sugar

Directions

In a blender, combine the bananas, ice cubes, milk and sugar. Cover, and blend for 2 minutes, or until ice is finely crushed.

Almond Banana Chocolate Muffins

Ingredients

1 (14 ounce) box banana quick bread and muffin mix, such as the Pillsbury® brand
1 cup water
2 eggs
1/4 cup vegetable oil
1/4 cup cinnamon-flavored applesauce
1 medium banana, diced
1 cup sliced California Almonds, divided
3/4 cup semi-sweet chocolate chips or chopped dark chocolate

Directions

Preheat oven to 400 degrees F. Prepare a muffin tin with paper liners.

Prepare muffins according to package instructions using water, eggs and oil, but use only 1/4 cup oil instead of 1/2 cup, and add 1/4 cup applesauce. Stir in banana, 3/4 cup almonds and chocolate. Divide evenly among muffin cups and sprinkle with remaining 1/4 cup almonds.

Bake 15-20 minutes, until a tester comes out clean. Cool muffin tin on a rack for 10 minutes, then remove muffins and continue cooling on rack. Store air tight at room temperature for up to 4 days.

Whole Wheat Banana Bread

Ingredients

1 cup whole wheat flour
3/4 cup all-purpose flour
1/2 cup toasted wheat germ
1 teaspoon baking soda
1 teaspoon grated orange peel
1/4 teaspoon salt
4 medium navel oranges, peeled and sectioned
2 medium ripe bananas
1 cup sugar
2 eggs
1/4 cup canola oil
1 teaspoon vanilla extract
1/2 cup chopped pecans

Directions

In a large bowl, combine the first six ingredients. In a food processor or blender, process the oranges, bananas, sugar, eggs, oil and vanilla until smooth. Stir into dry ingredients just until moistened. Fold in pecans.

Pour into two 8-in. x 4-in. x 2-in. loaf pans coated with nonstick cooking spray. Bake at 350 degrees F for 45-50 minutes or until a toothpick inserted near the center comes out clean. Cool for 10 minutes before removing from pans to wire racks to cool completely.

Peanut Butter Banana Oatmeal Raisin

Ingredients

1 banana, peeled and mashed
1 cup peanut butter
1/2 cup white sugar
1/2 cup packed brown sugar
2 egg whites
2 cups whole wheat flour
1 teaspoon baking soda
1 cup rolled oats
1 cup raisins

Directions

Preheat oven to 300 degrees F (150 degrees C).

In a medium bowl, stir together mashed banana, peanut butter, white sugar and brown sugar until smooth. Then mix in the egg whites. Add flour and baking soda, mix until just blended, then stir in the rolled oats and raisins.

Drop cookie dough by heaping spoonfuls onto an unprepared cookie sheet. Bake for 15 to 17 minutes in the preheated oven. When cookies are done, remove from the baking sheet and cool on wire racks.

Maple Walnut Banana Bread

Ingredients

1 3/4 cups all-purpose flour
1/3 cup sugar
1/3 cup packed brown sugar
2 teaspoons baking powder
1/2 teaspoon baking soda
1/4 teaspoon salt
2 eggs
1 cup mashed ripe banana
3 tablespoons butter or stick margarine, melted
2 tablespoons fat-free milk
1/4 teaspoon maple flavored extract
1/4 cup chopped walnuts

Directions

In a bowl, combine the first six ingredients. Combine the eggs, bananas, butter, milk and flavoring; mix well. Stir into dry ingredients just until moistened. Spoon into an 8-in. x 4-in. x 2-in. loaf pan coated with nonstick cooking spray. Sprinkle with walnuts.

Bake at 350 degrees F for 50-55 minutes or until a toothpick inserted near the center comes out clean. Cool for 10 minutes before removing from pan to a wire rack.

Banana Rum Cake

Ingredients

1 (18.25 ounce) package yellow cake mix
1/4 teaspoon baking soda
2/3 cup dark rum
2/3 cup water
2 eggs
1 cup mashed bananas
1/3 cup chopped pecans

1/3 cup butter, softened
3 cups confectioners' sugar
2 teaspoons vanilla extract
2 tablespoons dark rum

Directions

Preheat oven to 350 degrees F (175 degrees C). Grease and flour two 9-inch cake pans.

In a large bowl, combine cake mix, baking soda, rum, water, eggs, bananas and nuts. Bring together, then beat on medium speed 2 to 4 minutes.

Divide into prepared pans. Bake at 350 degrees F (175 degrees C) for 25 to 30 minutes, or until toothpick inserted into center of cake comes out clean. Cool completely.

For the frosting: Combine 1/3 cup butter or margarine with the confectioners sugar. Blend thoroughly. Stir in vanilla and 2 tablespoons rum. Beat until smooth.

Black-Bottom Banana Cream Pie

Ingredients

6 tablespoons butter or margarine, divided
25 NILLA Wafers, finely crushed
2 tablespoons sugar
4 (1 ounce) squares BAKER'S Semi-Sweet Baking Chocolate
2 large bananas, sliced
1 pkg. (4 serving size) JELL-O Vanilla Flavor Instant Pudding &Pie Filling
1 3/4 cups cold milk
1 cup thawed COOL WHIP Whipped Topping

Directions

Melt 1/4 cup (4 Tbsp.) of the butter; place in medium bowl. Add wafer crumbs and sugar; mix well. Remove 2 Tbsp. of the crumb mixture; set aside for later use. Press remaining crumb mixture firmly onto bottom and up side of 9-inch pie plate; set aside.

Microwave chocolate and remaining 2 Tbsp. butter in microwaveable bowl on HIGH 1 min. or until butter is melted; stir until chocolate is completely melted. Drizzle evenly onto bottom of crust; top with bananas. Set aside.

Prepare dry pudding mix with 1-3/4 cups cold milk as directed on package for pie; pour evenly over bananas. Refrigerate at least 4 hours or up to 24 hours. Top with whipped topping just before serving; sprinkle with reserved 2 Tbsp. crumb mixture. Store leftover pie in refrigerator.

Grape Banana Salad

Ingredients

1 pint heavy whipping cream
6 cups seedless red grapes, halved
4 large bananas, peeled and sliced
1 cup chopped walnuts

Directions

In a large bowl, beat the cream until stiff peaks form. Gently stir in fruit and nuts.

Chocolate Banana Latte Shake

Ingredients

1/2 cup milk
1/2 cup cold coffee
1 banana
3 tablespoons vanilla ice cream
3 tablespoons chocolate syrup
2 cups crushed ice

Directions

Combine the milk, coffee, banana, ice cream, chocolate syrup, and ice in a blender; blend until smooth.

Banana Bran Muffins

Ingredients

1 1/2 cups all-purpose flour
1 cup oat bran
1/2 cup whole wheat flour
1 tablespoon ground cinnamon
2 teaspoons baking powder
2 teaspoons baking soda 1/2
teaspoon ground nutmeg 1/4
teaspoon allspice
2 eggs
1 cup orange juice
1/2 cup sugar
1/2 cup packed brown sugar
1/2 cup vegetable oil
1 cup mashed ripe bananas
1/2 cup chopped walnuts

Directions

In a large bowl, combine the first eight ingredients. In another bowl, beat the eggs, juice, sugars and oil. Stir into dry ingredients just until moistened. Fold in bananas and nuts. Fill greased or paper-lined muffin cups two-thirds full. Bake at 400 degrees F for 15-18 minutes or until a toothpick comes out clean. Cool for 5 minutes before removing from pans to wire racks. Serve warm.

Banana Cream Pie V

Ingredients

1 (9 inch) deep dish pie crust, baked and cooled
2/3 cup white sugar
1/4 cup cornstarch
1/2 teaspoon salt
3 cups milk
4 egg yolks, beaten
2 tablespoons butter
1 large banana, sliced

4 egg whites
1/4 teaspoon cream of tartar
1/2 cup white sugar
1/4 teaspoon vanilla extract

Directions

In a large saucepan or double boiler combine sugar, cornstarch and salt. Mix well, then stir in milk and egg yolks. Whisk until all ingredients are thoroughly combined. Cook over medium heat, stirring constantly, until mixture is thickened. Remove from heat and stir in butter and 1 tablespoon vanilla.

Preheat oven to 400 degrees F (200 degrees C.) Pour half of custard into baked pie shell. Cover with sliced banana. Spread remaining custard over banana layer.

In a large glass or metal mixing bowl, beat egg whites and cream of tartar until foamy. Gradually add white sugar, continuing to beat until stiff peaks form. Spread meringue over pie, covering completely.

Bake in the preheated oven for 10 to 15 minutes, or until lightly browned.

Napoleon's Banana Muffin

Ingredients

6 very ripe bananas, mashed
1/2 cup brown sugar
1/4 cup honey
1/4 cup spiced rum
1/4 cup cognac
3 cups all-purpose flour
1 teaspoon baking soda
2 teaspoons baking powder
1 teaspoon salt
1 1/2 cups white sugar
2/3 cup brown sugar
2 eggs, lightly beaten
10 tablespoons unsalted butter, melted
3 tablespoons butter
1 cup brown sugar
3 tablespoons all-purpose flour
2 teaspoons ground cinnamon

Directions

Preheat the oven to 375 degrees F (190 degrees C). Grease two twelve-cup muffin tins.

In a mixing bowl, mix bananas, 1/2 cup brown sugar, honey, rum, and cognac with an electric mixer until smooth.

In a large bowl, whisk together 3 cups flour, baking soda, baking powder, and salt. In another bowl, cream white sugar, 2/3 cup brown sugar, eggs, and melted butter. Pour banana mixture and creamed egg mixture into the flour, and stir until just combined. Spoon mixture into muffin tins, filling cups 3/4 full.

In a small bowl, mix together 1 cup brown sugar, 3 tablespoons flour, and cinnamon. Cut in 3 tablespoons butter until mixture resembles coarse crumbs. Sprinkle over batter in muffin tins.

Bake muffins in preheated oven for 20 minutes, or until done.

Banana Pudding I

Ingredients

2/3 cup white sugar 1/3
cup all-purpose flour 1/4
teaspoon salt
3 eggs, beaten
2 cups milk
1/2 teaspoon vanilla extract
2 tablespoons butter, softened
2 bananas, peeled and sliced
1/2 (12 ounce) package vanilla
wafer cookies

Directions

In medium saucepan combine sugar, flour and salt. Add eggs and stir well. Stir in milk, and cook over low heat, stirring constantly. When mixture begins to thicken, remove from heat and continue to stir, cooling slightly. Stir in vanilla and butter until smooth.

In 9x13-inch dish, layer pudding with bananas and vanilla wafers. Chill at least one hour in refrigerator before serving.

Banana Split Cookies

Ingredients

1/2 cup butter
1 cup packed brown sugar
2 eggs
1 cup mashed bananas
2 cups all-purpose flour
2 teaspoons baking powder
1/4 teaspoon baking soda
1/4 teaspoon salt
1/2 teaspoon ground cinnamon
1/4 teaspoon ground cloves
1/2 cup chopped walnuts

Directions

In a medium bowl, cream together the butter and brown sugar. Beat in the eggs and mashed banana. Sift together the flour, baking powder, baking soda, salt, cinnamon, and cloves; blend into the banana mixture. Stir in the nuts. Cover, and chill for at least 1 hour.

Preheat the oven to 375 degrees F (190 degrees C). Lightly grease cookie sheets. Drop dough by rounded teaspoons onto the prepared cookie sheets.

Bake for 8 to 10 minutes in the preheated oven, or until no imprint remains when touched. Cool on wire racks.

Surprise Banana Cake

Ingredients

1 cup white sugar
1/2 cup unsalted butter
2 eggs
4 ripe bananas, mashed
2 cups all-purpose flour
1 teaspoon baking soda
1/2 teaspoon salt
1/2 cup chopped walnuts
1 teaspoon vanilla extract

Directions

Preheat oven to 375 degrees F (190 degrees C). Grease and flour one 9 x 13 inch cake pan.

Cream together the butter or margarine and the sugar.

Add eggs, bananas, flour, soda, salt, nuts, and vanilla. Mix thoroughly and pour batter into the prepared pan.

Bake at 375 degrees F (190 degrees C) for 30 minutes. Cool and frost cake.

Delicious Sour Cream-Banana Bread

Ingredients

1/4 cup butter, softened
1 cup sugar
1 cup mashed fully ripe bananas
1 cup KNUDSEN Sour Cream
2 eggs
2 1/4 cups flour
1 1/2 teaspoons baking powder
1/2 teaspoon baking soda
1/2 teaspoon salt
1 cup chopped walnuts

Directions

Heat oven to 350 degrees F.

Beat butter and sugar in large bowl with mixer until well blended. Add bananas, sour cream and eggs; mix well. Add combined dry ingredients; mix just until moistened. Stir in nuts. Pour into greased and floured 9x5-inch loaf pan.

Bake 1 hour or until toothpick inserted in center comes out clean.

Cool 5 min.; remove from pan to wire rack. Cool completely before slicing to serve. Refrigerate leftovers.

Peaches 'N Cream Banana Breakfast Smoothie

Ingredients

1 1/4 cups milk
1/4 cup vanilla yogurt
1 banana, broken into chunks
1 packet peaches and cream flavor instant oatmeal
2 packets granular no-calorie sucralose sweetener (such as Splenda®) (optional)
5 ice cubes

Directions

Place the milk, yogurt, banana, instant oatmeal, sweetener, and ice cubes into a blender. Cover, and puree until smooth. Pour into glasses to serve.

Banana Pudding Cake

Ingredients

1 (18.25 ounce) package yellow cake mix
1 (3.5 ounce) package instant banana pudding mix
4 eggs
1 cup water
1/4 cup vegetable oil
3/4 cup mashed bananas

2 cups confectioners' sugar
2 tablespoons milk
1 dash vanilla extract
1/2 cup chopped walnuts (optional)

Directions

Preheat oven to 350 degrees F (175 degrees C). Grease and flour a 10 inch Bundt pan.

In a large bowl, stir together cake mix and pudding mix. Make a well in the center and pour in eggs, water, oil and mashed banana. Beat on low speed until blended. Scrape bowl, and beat 4 minutes on medium speed. Pour batter into prepared pan.

Bake in a preheated oven for 50 to 55 minutes, or until cake tests done. Let cool in pan for 10 minutes, then turn out onto a wire rack and cool completely.

To make glaze: In a small bowl, combine confectioners' sugar, milk and vanilla. Whisk until smooth and of a drizzling consistency. When cake is cooled, drizzle icing over cake with a zigzag motion. Sprinkle chopped nuts over wet icing if desired.

Orange Banana Smoothie

Ingredients

1 cup cold milk
2 oranges, peeled and segmented
1 banana
1/4 cup sugar
1 pinch salt
1/2 (8 ounce) container vanilla fatfree yogurt
4 cubes ice

Directions

In a blender, combine milk, oranges, banana, sugar, salt and yogurt. Blend for about 1 minute. Insert ice cubes, and blend until smooth. Pour into glasses and serve.

Banana Pudding with Meringue

Ingredients

1 cup packed brown sugar 1
egg
2 egg yolks
1 tablespoon all-purpose flour
1 1/2 cups milk
6 bananas, peeled and sliced
1 (16 ounce) package vanilla wafer
cookies
2 egg whites
3 1/2 tablespoons white sugar

Directions

Preheat the oven to 425 degrees F (220 degrees C).

Line the bottom of a 1 1/2 quart casserole dish with vanilla wafer cookies. Top with a layer of banana slices. Repeat layers until you reach the top of the dish or run out of bananas. Set aside.

In a large saucepan, stir together the brown sugar and flour so there are no lumps. Mix in the egg and egg yolks. Gradually stir in the milk while warming over low heat, stirring constantly until the mixture becomes thick enough to coat the back of a metal spoon. Remove from the heat and allow to cool for about 1 minute. Then, pour the hot pudding evenly over the layers of banana and cookie in the casserole dish.

In a separate clean bowl, whip the egg whites with an electric mixer until they can hold a soft peak. Gradually sprinkle in the sugar while continuing to whip until they can hold a firm peak. Use a spatula to spread the meringue over the top of the casserole.

Bake in the preheated oven until the meringue has browned, 5 to 10 minutes. Serve warm or at room temperature.

Banana-Orange Smoothie

Ingredients

1 banana, peeled
1 large orange, peeled and seeded
2 cups vanilla-flavored soy milk
1 teaspoon ground ginger

Directions

Place banana, orange, soy milk, and ginger in an electric blender. Process until ingredients are blended and smooth.

Cranberry Banana Coffee Cake

Ingredients

1/2 cup butter or margarine, softened
1/2 cup sugar
2 eggs
1 teaspoon vanilla extract
2 cups all-purpose flour
2 teaspoons baking powder
1 teaspoon ground cinnamon
1/4 teaspoon salt
1/4 teaspoon ground allspice
2 medium ripe bananas, mashed
1 cup whole berry cranberry sauce
TOPPING:
1/2 cup packed brown sugar
1/2 cup chopped pecans
2 tablespoons all-purpose flour
2 tablespoons butter or margarine, melted

Directions

In a large mixing bowl, cream the butter and sugar. Beat in eggs and vanilla. Combine the dry ingredients; add to the creamed mixture alternately with bananas. Spread into a greased 13-in. x 9-in. x 2-in. baking pan. Top with cranberry sauce.

In a small bowl, combine brown sugar, pecans and flour; stir in butter. Sprinkle over cranberries. Bake at 350 degrees F for 45-50 minutes or until a toothpick inserted near the center comes out clean. Cool in pan on a wire rack.

Banana Praline Muffins

Ingredients

1/3 cup chopped pecans
3 tablespoons brown sugar
1 tablespoon sour cream
1 egg, lightly beaten
3 small ripe bananas, mashed
1/2 cup sugar
1/4 cup vegetable oil
1 1/2 cups packaged pancake mix

Directions

In a small bowl, combine pecans, brown sugar and sour cream; set aside. Combine egg, bananas, sugar and oil; mix well. Stir in pancake mix just until moistened. Fill greased or paper-lined muffin cups two-thirds full. Drop 1 teaspoon of pecan mixture into center of each muffin. Bake at 400 degrees F for 15-20 minutes or until muffins test done.

Banana Wake-Up Bars

Ingredients

1/3 cup peanut butter
1/3 cup brown sugar
2 1/2 tablespoons butter
1 egg
1/2 teaspoon vanilla extract
1 ripe banana, mashed
2/3 cup rolled oats
1/3 cup all-purpose flour
2 tablespoons wheat germ
1/4 teaspoon baking soda

Directions

Preheat oven to 350 degrees F (175 degrees C). Grease a 9x9-inch baking pan.

In a mixing bowl, beat together the peanut butter, brown sugar, and butter with an electric mixer until smooth and fluffy. Beat in the egg and vanilla extract, then the banana. Stir in the oats, flour, wheat germ, and baking soda until completely combined. Spread in prepared baking pan.

Bake in the preheated oven until set and lightly browned, 20 to 25 minutes. Remove from oven and cool in pan on wire rack before cutting into bars.

Banana Blondie

Ingredients

2 cups all-purpose flour
1 cup white sugar
6 packets aspartame artificial sweetener
1 1/2 teaspoons baking powder
3/4 teaspoon baking soda
1/2 cup butter, melted
1 tablespoon vanilla extract
3/4 cup skim milk
2 eggs
4 ripe bananas, mashed

Directions

Preheat the oven to 350 degrees F (175 degrees C). Grease a 9x13 inch baking dish.

In a large bowl, stir together the flour, sugar, artificial sweetener, baking powder and baking soda. In a separate bowl, stir together the butter, vanilla, milk, eggs and bananas; pour into the dry ingredients and mix well. Spread evenly in the prepared pan.

Bake for 35 minutes in the preheated oven, until a toothpick inserted in the center comes out clean.

Banana Cake X

Ingredients

2 tablespoons lemon juice
2/3 cup milk
2 large very ripe bananas, mashed
1 (18.25 ounce) package butter cake mix
1 teaspoon baking soda
1/2 cup butter, softened
3 eggs
1 teaspoon vanilla extract

Directions

Preheat oven to 350 degrees F (175 degrees C). Grease and flour a 9x13 inch pan. Put 1 tablespoon lemon juice in a measuring cup with 2/3 cup milk. Set aside. Mash bananas with a fork, adding the remaining 1 tablespoon lemon juice to them as you mash. Set aside.

In a large bowl, combine cake mix and baking soda. Stir to combine. Add bananas, softened butter, milk mixture, eggs and vanilla. Beat at low speed until moistened (about 30 seconds). Beat at medium speed for 4 minutes. Pour into prepared pan.

Bake in the preheated oven for 30 to 35 minutes, or until center of cake springs back when lightly tapped. A toothpick stuck in the center may leave a slight crumb. Allow to cool on a wire rack.

Peanut Butter, Berry & Banana Stuffed French

Ingredients

1/4   cup
SMUCKER'SB®Strawber
ry Fruit Syurp
1/4 cup JIFB® Creamy Peanut
Butter
2 ounces cream cheese, softened
8 slices Italian bread
2 medium bananas, cut in slices
about 1/4-inch thick
4 large eggs
1/4 cup milk
1 tablespoon butter
SMUCKER'SB® Strawberry Fruit
Syurp
Whipped cream (optional)

Directions

Stir together fruit syrup and peanut butter until smooth. Add softened cream cheese. Stir until blended. Spread mixture evenly on 8 slices of bread. Place banana slices on top of 4 slices of bread. Top with peanut butter covered bread slices to make 4 sandwiches.

Whisk together eggs and milk in a shallow bowl.

Melt butter in skillet or on griddle over medium heat.

Dip both sides of each "sandwich" in egg mixture, letting it soak in slightly. Cook in hot skillet or on griddle, 2 minutes or until golden brown. Turn, cooking another 2 minutes or until golden.

Serve immediately topped with additional strawberry syrup and whipped cream, if desired.

Banana Pudding Sugar Cookies

Ingredients

2/3 cup shortening
2/3 cup white sugar
2 eggs
1 teaspoon vanilla extract 1/2
teaspoon baking powder 1/2
teaspoon salt
1 (3.5 ounce) package instant
banana pudding mix
2 1/2 cups all-purpose flour

Directions

In a medium bowl, cream together shortening and sugar until light and fluffy. Beat in eggs one at a time. Stir in vanilla extract, baking powder, salt, and instant banana pudding mix. Mix in 2 cups flour. Gradually mix in remaining 1/2 cup flour as needed to form a workable dough. Cover, and chill in the refrigerator at least 2 hours.

Preheat oven to 375 degrees F (190 degrees C). Grease baking sheets. Shape dough into walnut sized balls, and place 2 inches apart on the prepared baking sheets. Flatten balls to a thickness of about 1/4 inch.

Bake 8 to 10 minutes in the preheated oven, or until lightly browned.

Creamy Banana Lettuce Salad

Ingredients

1 large firm banana, sliced
1/2 teaspoon lemon juice
3 tablespoons mayonnaise
1/2 teaspoon sugar
2 cups torn mixed salad greens
5 fresh strawberries, sliced
1 tablespoon salted peanuts, chopped

Directions

Lightly toss banana slices with lemon juice. Place 1/4 cup in a small bowl; mash. Stir in the mayonnaise and sugar. In a salad bowl, combine the greens, strawberries and remaining banana slices; toss. Top with banana dressing; sprinkle with peanuts.

Strawberry Banana Dessert

Ingredients

3 medium firm bananas, sliced
1 (16 ounce) package angel food cake mix, prepared and cut into 1-inch cubes
1 pint fresh strawberries, halved
1 (.6 ounce) package sugar-free strawberry gelatin
2 cups boiling water
1 1/2 cups cold water
1 (8 ounce) tub reduced-fat whipped topping

Directions

Layer banana slices and cake cubes in a 13-in. x 9-in. x 2-in. dish coated with nonstick cooking spray. Place strawberries over cake and press down gently. In a bowl, dissolve gelatin in boiling water; stir in cold water. Pour over strawberries. Refrigerate for 3 hours or until set. Frost with whipped topping.

Tropical Baked Bananas

Ingredients

1/4 cup butter, softened
1/3 cup brown sugar
1/4 teaspoon ground cloves
1 1/2 teaspoons orange juice
6 bananas, peeled and halved lengthwise
1/3 cup shredded coconut

Directions

Preheat oven to 375 degrees F (190 degrees C). Grease a 7x11 inch baking dish.

In a small bowl, cream together butter and sugar. Stir in cloves and orange juice until smooth. Place the bananas in the prepared dish and spread the butter mixture evenly over the bananas. Sprinkle with coconut.

Bake in preheated oven until bubbly and heated through, 10 minutes.

Chicken and Coconut in Banana Leaves

Ingredients

1 teaspoon low-sodium soy sauce
1 teaspoon barbeque sauce
1 teaspoon minced fresh ginger
3/4 cup coconut milk
2 chicken drumsticks
2 chicken thighs
2 yellow plantains, peeled and cut into 3/4 inch slices
1 sweet potato, peeled and cut into thick sticks
1 fresh, unsplit banana leaf

Directions

Whisk together soy sauce, barbeque sauce, ginger, and coconut. Pour over chicken drumsticks, thighs, plantain, and sweet potato in a resealable plastic bag. Seal, and marinate 30 minutes.

Preheat oven to 350 degrees F (175 degrees C).

Gently warm the whole banana leaf over a fire or gas burner until the leaf is pliable, but not burnt, 3 to 4 minutes. Cut the leaf into four large squares, measuring at least 12x12 inches. Carefully cut four long, thin strips from the rib of the leaf, these will be used as 'string' to tie the packets later.

Place a piece of meat onto each banana leaf square, and evenly divide the vegetables on top. Pour in any remaining marinade, and fold the leaves around the chicken like a present. Securely tie with the rib strips, and place the packets onto a baking sheet.

Bake in preheated oven until the chicken is tender and no longer pink in the center, about 1 hour. Check the packets occasionally to make sure they do not burn.

Apple-Banana Oatmeal

Ingredients

1 cup water
1 tablespoon orange juice concentrate
1/2 cup chopped unpeeled tart apple
1/4 cup sliced firm banana
1/4 cup raisins
1/4 teaspoon salt (optional)
1/8 teaspoon ground cinnamon
2/3 cup quick-cooking oats
1/3 cup oat bran
brown sugar (optional)

Directions

In a saucepan, combine water, orange juice concentrate, apple, banana, raisins, salt if desired and cinnamon; bring to a boil. Stir in oats and oat bran. Cook for 1-2 minutes, stirring occasionally. Sprinkle with brown sugar if desired.

Hawaiian Banana Bars

Ingredients

1/4 cup shortening
1/2 teaspoon vanilla extract
1 cup mashed bananas
1/2 cup chopped walnuts
1 1/2 teaspoons baking powder
1 cup packed brown sugar
1/2 teaspoon lemon juice
1 1/2 cups all-purpose flour
1/2 teaspoon salt
1/3 cup confectioners' sugar
1 teaspoon ground cinnamon

Directions

Preheat oven to 350 degrees F (175 degrees C). Grease an 11x7 inch pan.

In large mixing bowl, mix shortening, brown sugar, vanilla, lemon juice and banana until well blended.

Sift together the flour, baking powder and salt. Add to the banana mixture; stir until well blended. Stir in chopped nuts. Pour into the prepared pan.

Bake for 30 to 35 minutes in the preheated oven.

While warm, cut into bars and remove from pan. Combine powdered sugar and cinnamon. Gently roll warm bars in sugar-cinnamon mixture.

Best Ever Banana Bread

Ingredients

2 eggs, beaten
1/3 cup buttermilk
1/2 cup vegetable oil
1 cup mashed bananas
1 1/2 cups white sugar
1 3/4 cups all-purpose flour
1 teaspoon baking soda
1/2 teaspoon salt
1/2 cup chopped pecans
(optional)

Directions

Preheat oven to 325 degrees F (165 degrees C). Spray one 9x5 inch loaf pan with non-stick spray coating.

Blend together the eggs, buttermilk, oil and bananas.

Sift together the sugar, flour, baking soda and salt. Add to banana mixture and stir in pecans. Mix well.

Pour into prepared loaf pan and bake 1 hour and 20 minutes or until a cake tester inserted in the center comes out clean.

Banana Cookies

Ingredients

2 1/4 cups all-purpose flour
2 teaspoons baking powder
1/2 teaspoon salt
1/3 cup shortening
1 cup white sugar
2 eggs
1/2 teaspoon vanilla extract
1/4 teaspoon lemon extract
3 ripe bananas, mashed
1/2 cup ground walnuts

Directions

Preheat oven to 350 degrees F (175 degrees C). Lightly grease or line baking sheets with parchment paper.

In a large bowl cream the shortening and the sugar together. Beat in the eggs, vanilla and lemon extract. Beat in the bananas and the nuts. Gradually add the flour, baking powder and salt.

Drop the dough by spoonfuls onto the prepared baking sheets. Bake at 350 degrees F (175 degrees C) for 12 to 15 minutes or until lightly colored. Transfer to wire racks to cool.

Peanut Butter Banana Bread

Ingredients

1/2 cup butter, softened
1 cup sugar
2 eggs
1 cup mashed ripe banana
3/4 cup chunky peanut butter
2 cups all-purpose flour
1 teaspoon salt
1 teaspoon baking soda

Directions

In a mixing bowl, cream butter and sugar. Add eggs, one at a time, beating well after each addition. Add bananas and peanut butter; mix well. Combine the flour, salt and baking soda; add to creamed mixture.

Transfer to a greased 9-in. x 5-in. x 3-in. loaf ban. Bake at 350 degrees F for 70-75 minutes or until toothpick inserted near the center comes out clean. Cool for 10 minutes before removing from pan to a wire rack to cool completely.

Banana Oatmeal Cookies

Ingredients

1 cup sugar
1 cup butter flavored shortening
2 eggs
1 teaspoon vanilla extract
2 cups all-purpose flour
1 teaspoon baking soda
1 teaspoon ground cloves
1 teaspoon ground cinnamon
3 medium bananas, mashed
2 cups quick-cooking oats
1 cup semisweet chocolate chips

Directions

In a large bowl, cream sugar, shortening, eggs and vanilla. Combine flour, baking soda, cloves and cinnamon; add to creamed mixture. Stir in bananas, oats and chocolate chips. Drop by rounded teaspoonfuls onto greased baking sheets. Bake at 375 degrees F for 10-12 minutes. Immediately remove cookies to wire racks to cool.

Banana Chocolate Chip Cake

Ingredients

1 1/2 cups all-purpose flour
2/3 cup white sugar
1 1/2 teaspoons baking powder
1/4 teaspoon salt
1 cup mashed bananas
1 egg
1/2 cup unsalted butter, melted
1/4 cup milk
3/4 cup semisweet chocolate chips

Directions

Preheat oven to 350 degrees F (175 degrees C). Grease and flour a 9x13 inch pan.

In a large bowl, mix flour, sugar, baking powder and salt.

In a separate bowl, combine bananas, egg, melted butter and milk.

Stir banana mixture into flour mixture until blended. Be careful not to over mix.

Stir in chocolate chips.

Pour batter into 9x13 inch pan. Bake at 350 degrees F (175 degrees C) 30 to 35 minutes, or until a toothpick inserted into center of cake comes out clean. (It will have some melted chocolate, but no crumbs.)

Banana Meatloaf

Ingredients

1 pound lean ground beef
1 cup fresh bread crumbs
1 tablespoon minced onion
3/4 cup mashed banana 1/2
teaspoon salt
1/8 teaspoon ground black
pepper
1/4 teaspoon paprika
1/2 teaspoon ground mustard

Directions

Preheat oven to 350 degrees F (175 degrees C). Grease a 9x5 inch loaf pan.

In a large bowl, combine ground beef, bread crumbs, onion, banana, salt, pepper, paprika and dry mustard until well mixed. Shape into a loaf and place in prepared pan.

Bake in preheated oven 1 hour, or until no longer pink in the center.

Banana Flavored Jam

Ingredients

4 cups mashed ripe bananas
1/3 cup fresh lemon juice
2 tablespoons brown sugar
1/4 teaspoon ground nutmeg

Directions

Combine all ingredients in a blender and puree until smooth. Heat to a boiling in a saucepan and simmer slowly, till mixture is thickened. Serve warm over pancakes or cool and serve as a jam.

Banana Split Cake I

Ingredients

2 cups graham cracker crumbs
1/2 cup melted butter
2 cups confectioners' sugar
2 eggs
1 cup butter, softened
6 bananas, peeled and halved lengthwise
1 (20 ounce) can crushed pineapple, drained
1 quart fresh strawberries, halved
1 (16 ounce) package frozen whipped topping, thawed
1 cup chopped walnuts

Directions

Combine cracker crumbs and melted butter or margarine thoroughly and press into bottom of 9x12 inch baking pan. Chill in freezer for at least 15 minutes.

In the medium bowl of an electric mixer combine confectioners sugar, eggs, and softened butter or margarine; beat at medium speed for 20 minutes. (This step is important, so don't try to save time).

Spread buttercream mixture evenly over chilled crust. Place bananas, cut side down, evenly on top of buttercream and spoon crushed pineapple evenly over top of bananas. Distribute strawberries over pineapple and spread the whipped topping evenly all over. Sprinkle with walnuts and refrigerate for at least 3 hours or overnight before serving.

Pineapple Banana Shakes

Ingredients

1 (8 ounce) can crushed pineapple, undrained
1 medium firm banana, quartered
1 cup buttermilk
1 tablespoon honey
1/8 teaspoon coconut extract

Directions

In a food processor or blender, combine all ingredients; cover and process until smooth. Pour into glasses; serve immediately.

Banana Drops

Ingredients

2 1/2 cups all-purpose flour
1/4 teaspoon baking soda
1/4 teaspoon salt
7/8 cup brown sugar
1/4 teaspoon ground cinnamon
1/2 cup butter
1/4 teaspoon vanilla extract
1/4 teaspoon banana extract
2 eggs
3 ripe bananas, mashed
1/3 cup chopped walnuts, toasted

Directions

Preheat oven to 400 degrees F (200 degrees C). Line a cookie sheet with parchment paper.

In a medium size mixing bowl, sift together flour, baking soda and salt. In a separate small bowl, combine 2 tablespoons brown sugar with cinnamon, set aside.

In a medium size mixing bowl, beat together 3/4 cup brown sugar with the butter or margarine, vanilla and banana extract until the mixture is light in texture. Beat in the eggs. Mix in the banana. Slowly mix the flour mixture into the egg, banana and sugar mixture. Fold in nuts. Drop the dough by teaspoonful onto the prepared cookie sheet. Sprinkle the cookies with the mixture of brown sugar and cinnamon prepared earlier.

Bake 8 to 10 minutes, until lightly browned.

Banana Peanut Butter Bread

Ingredients

1/2 cup butter, softened
1 cup white sugar
2 eggs
1/2 cup peanut butter
2 bananas, mashed
2 cups all-purpose flour
1 teaspoon baking soda
1/2 cup chopped walnuts

Directions

Preheat oven to 325 degrees F (165 degrees C). Lightly grease a 5x9 inch loaf pan.

In a large mixing bowl, cream together butter and sugar. Add eggs; beat well. Stir in peanut butter, bananas, flour and baking soda until blended. Fold in walnuts. Pour into prepared pan.

Bake at 325 degrees F (165 degrees C) for 70 minutes, or until a toothpick inserted into center of the loaf comes out clean. Remove to a wire rack to cool.

Banana Blast II

Ingredients

2 bananas
1 cup milk
1/4 cup water
2 tablespoons brown sugar
8 cubes ice

Directions

In a blender combine bananas and milk. Pulse until bananas are chopped. Pour in water and brown sugar. Blend until smooth. Toss in the Ice cubes and blend until smooth. Pour into 4 glasses and serve immediately.

Banana Cake V

Ingredients

1 1/4 cups white sugar
1/2 cup butter
2 eggs, beaten
1 teaspoon baking soda
1/4 cup sour cream
1 cup mashed bananas
1 1/2 cups cake flour
1 teaspoon vanilla extract

Directions

Preheat oven to 350 degrees F (175 degrees C). Grease and flour a 9x9 inch pan.

In a large bowl, cream butter and sugar until light. Add eggs and beat well. Dissolve soda in the sour cream and add it to the butter mixture. Beat well. Add the mashed bananas and mix in. Add cake flour and mix well. Stir in vanilla extract.

Pour batter into a 9x9 inch pan and bake at 350 degrees F (175 degrees C) for 45 minutes or until done.

Banana Bread III

Ingredients

3 tablespoons margarine
2 cups white sugar
3 egg yolks
3 cups all-purpose flour
1 tablespoon baking powder
1 cup milk
3 egg whites
6 bananas
2 tablespoons white sugar
1 teaspoon ground cinnamon

Directions

Preheat oven to 350 degrees F (175 degrees C). Grease a 9x13 inch pan.

In a large bowl, mix together margarine and sugar until smooth. Mix in yolks. Stir in flour and baking powder alternately with the milk.

In another bowl, beat egg whites until doubled in volume. Fold beaten whites into the dough. Spread into a greased 9 x 12 inch pan. Slice bananas over the top of the dough. In a small bowl, mix together the 2 tablespoons sugar and the cinnamon; sprinkle over bananas.

Bake at 350 degrees F (175 degrees C) for 30 to 35 minutes, or until a toothpick inserted into the center comes out clean. Allow to cool.

Brown Sugar Banana Nut Bread II

Ingredients

1/2 cup milk
2 tablespoons butter, softened
2 eggs
1/4 cup white sugar
1/4 cup brown sugar
1 1/2 cups all-purpose flour
1 teaspoon salt
1 teaspoon baking soda
1 (.25 ounce) package active dry yeast
2 small ripe bananas, sliced
1/2 cup chopped walnuts

Directions

Place ingredients in the pan of the bread machine in the order recommended by the manufacturer. Select cycle; press Start. If your machine has a Fruit setting, add the bananas and nuts at the signal, or about 5 minutes before the kneading cycle has finished.

Banana Chocolate Chip Cookies

Ingredients

2 1/2 cups all-purpose flour
2 teaspoons baking powder
1/2 teaspoon salt
1/4 teaspoon baking soda
1 cup white sugar
2/3 cup butter, softened
2 eggs
1 teaspoon vanilla extract
1 cup mashed bananas
2 cups semisweet chocolate chips

Directions

Preheat oven to 400 degrees F (200 degrees C). Grease cookie sheets. Sift the flour, baking powder, salt, and baking soda together, and set aside.

Cream the butter with the sugar until light and fluffy. Beat in the eggs and vanilla. Mix in the mashed bananas. Add the flour mixture, and stir until just combined. Stir in the chocolate chips. Drop by spoonfuls onto prepared cookie sheets.

Bake in preheated oven for 12 to 15 minutes.

Creamy Banana Pudding

Ingredients

1 (14 ounce) can EAGLE BRAND®Sweetened Condensed Milk
1 1/2 cups cold water
1 (4-serving size) package instant vanilla pudding mix
2 cups whipping cream, whipped
36 vanilla wafers
3 medium bananas, sliced and dipped in
lemon juice

Directions

In large bowl, combine sweetened condensed milk and water. Add pudding mix; beat until well blended. Chill 5 minutes.

Fold in whipped cream. Spoon 1 cup pudding mixture into 2 1/2-quart glass serving bowl.

Top with one-third each of the vanilla wafers, bananas and remaining pudding. Repeat layering twice, ending with pudding mixture. Chill thoroughly. Garnish as desired. Store leftovers covered in refrigerator.

Peanut Butter-Chocolate Banana Cream Pie

Ingredients

35 NILLA Wafers, finely crushed
1/4 cup butter, melted
2 medium bananas, halved lengthwise, quartered
2 squares BAKER"S Semi-Sweet Chocolate, divided
1/2 cup peanut butter
2 cups milk
2 pkg. (4 serving size) JELL-O Vanilla Flavor Instant Pudding
2 cups COOL WHIP Whipped Topping, divided
2 tablespoons PLANTERS Salted Peanuts, coarsely chopped

Directions

Preheat oven to 350 degrees F. Mix wafer crumbs and butter until well blended; press firmly onto bottom and up side of 9-inch pie plate. Bake 5 to 8 min. or until golden brown. Cool completely; top with bananas.

Make chocolate curls from 1/2 square of the chocolate; reserve for garnish. Microwave remaining chocolate and the peanut butter on HIGH 1 min.; stir until chocolate is completely melted and mixture is well blended. Drizzle over bananas; set aside. Pour milk into large bowl. Add dry pudding mixes. Beat with wire whisk 2 min. or until well blended. Gently stir in 1 cup of the whipped topping. Spread over bananas; top with remaining 1 cup whipped topping.

Refrigerate at least 3 hours or overnight. Top with chocolate curls and peanuts just before serving. Store leftover pie in refrigerator.

Banana Split Cake IV

Ingredients

2 cups graham cracker crumbs
1/2 cup butter, melted
1 (8 ounce) package cream cheese
1/4 cup butter, softened
3 cups confectioners' sugar
4 bananas
1 (20 ounce) can crushed pineapple, drained
1 quart strawberries, stemmed and quartered
1 1/2 cups sugar free strawberry glaze
1 (12 ounce) container lite frozen whipped topping, thawed
1 (10 ounce) jar maraschino cherries, drained and quartered

Directions

In a medium bowl, mix together the graham cracker crumbs and melted butter. Press into the bottom of a 9x13 inch baking pan. Chill to set.

In a large bowl, mix together the cream cheese, butter and confectioners' sugar until smooth and creamy. Spread over the chilled graham cracker crust. Arrange the sliced bananas over the cream cheese mixture. Then cover with the drained crushed pineapple. Place strawberries cut side down over the pineapple layer, then coat with the strawberry glaze. Spread the whipped topping over the strawberry layer, decorate with maraschino cherries and sprinkle with chopped nuts.

Refrigerate at least 4 hours before serving.

Chocolate Banana Cake

Ingredients

1 (18.25 ounce) package devil's food cake mix
1 cup mashed bananas
1/3 cup vegetable oil
3 eggs

Directions

Preheat oven to 350 degrees F (175 degrees C). Grease and flour one 13x9 inch pan.

Beat cake mix, mashed bananas, oil and eggs with an electric mixer on low speed for 30 seconds. Increase speed to medium and beat for 2 more minutes. Pour the batter into the prepared pan.

Bake at 350 degrees F (175 degrees C) for 33 to 36 minutes or untila toothpick inserted near the center comes out clean. Let cake cool then frost with your choice of frosting, if desired.

Patriotic Banana Split

Ingredients

4 ounces reduced fat cream cheese
1/2 cup marshmallow creme
1 tablespoon lemon juice
1 teaspoon grated lemon peel
1/2 medium seedless watermelon
6 large ripe bananas, quartered
1/3 cup fresh blueberries
1/3 cup reduced-fat granola cereal without raisins

Directions

In a mixing bowl, beat the cream cheese, marshmallow creme, lemon juice and peel until smooth; set aside. Using an ice cream scoop, scoop six balls from watermelon (save remaining melon for another use). In shallow dessert bowls, arrange four banana quarters; top with a watermelon ball. Spoon cream cheese topping over melon. Sprinkle with blueberries and cereal. Serve immediately.

Banana Layer Cake

Ingredients

3 tablespoons shortening
3/4 cup sugar
2 eggs, separated
1/2 cup mashed ripe banana
1 cup all-purpose flour
1 1/2 teaspoons baking powder
1/2 teaspoon salt
1/4 teaspoon baking soda
1/2 cup 1% buttermilk
FROSTING:
3 tablespoons shortening
3 tablespoons butter, softened
3 cups confectioners' sugar, divided
1/4 teaspoon salt
1/4 teaspoon lemon extract
1/3 cup mashed ripe banana
3 drops yellow food coloring

Directions

In a small mixing bowl, beat shortening and sugar until crumbly, about 2 minutes. Add egg yolks; beat well. Add banana; beat on low speed until blended. Combine the flour, baking powder, salt and baking soda; add to banana mixture alternately with buttermilk. In a small mixing bowl, beat egg whites until soft peaks form; fold into batter.

Coat two 6-in. round baking pans with nonstick cooking spray and dust with flour. Add batter. Bake at 375 degrees F for 23-25 minutes or until a toothpick inserted near the center comes out clean. Cool for 10 minutes before removing from pans to wire racks to cool completely.

For frosting, in a small mixing bowl, combine shortening and butter. Add 1/2 cup confectioners' sugar, salt and extract; mix well. Stir in banana. Beat in enough of the remaining confectioners' sugar to achieve desired spreading consistency. Tint with food coloring if desired. Spread between layers and over top and sides of cake. Store in the refrigerator.

Super Strawberry-Banana Cookies

Ingredients

1 (18.25 ounce) package strawberry cake mix
2 eggs
1/3 cup vegetable oil
1/3 cup confectioners' sugar for decoration
1 banana

Directions

Mix together the cake mix, eggs, and vegetable oil.

Drop by teaspoonful onto foil covered cookie sheet. Cook at 350 degrees F (175 degrees C) for 7 to 8 minutes. Do not overbake. (Overbaking will cause your cookies to be hard as rocks!)

Once your cookies are all done, lightly dust with confectioners' sugar. Place in container with the banana (leave the peel on), and cover with the foil from the baking sheet. After a couple of hours, or overnight, the cookies will take on some of the banana flavor and taste great! I discovered this by accident when I sent the strawberry cookies and a banana together for the dessert in my husband's lunch!

Banana Blueberry Muffins

Ingredients

2 cups whole wheat flour
1/3 cup brown sugar
1/2 teaspoon ground cinnamon
2 teaspoons baking powder
1 teaspoon baking soda
1 1/2 cups mashed bananas
4 egg whites
1 teaspoon vanilla extract
1 cup fresh blueberries

Directions

Preheat oven to 350 degrees F (175 degrees C). Lightly grease a 12 cup muffin pan.

In a large bowl, mix the whole wheat flour, brown sugar, cinnamon, baking powder, and baking soda. In a separate bowl, mix the bananas, egg whites, and vanilla extract.

Mix the banana mixture into the flour mixture until smooth. Fold in the blueberries. Spoon the batter into the prepared muffin pan.

Bake 16 minutes in the preheated oven, or until a toothpick inserted in the center of a muffin comes out clean.

Banana Boats

Ingredients

4 medium unpeeled ripe bananas
2 tablespoons flaked coconut
2 tablespoons chopped maraschino cherries
2 tablespoons raisins
2 tablespoons peanut butter chips
1/2 cup miniature marshmallows

Directions

Cut banana peels lengthwise about 1/2 in. deep and to within 1/2 in. of each end. Open peel to form a pocket. Combine coconut and cherries; spoon into pockets of two bananas. Combine raisins and peanut butter chips; fill remaining bananas. Divide marshmallow between bananas. Wrap each in an 18-in. x 12-in. piece of heavy-duty foil. Grill, uncovered, over medium heat for 10-15 minutes or until marshmallows are melted and golden brown.

Elegant White Chocolate Banana Cream Pie

Ingredients

1 (9 inch) pie crust, baked
6 egg yolks, beaten
5 tablespoons white sugar
1/4 cup sifted cornstarch
2 cups milk
1 vanilla bean, halved
2 tablespoons butter, diced
3 ounces white chocolate, melted
8 ripe bananas
1 lemon, juiced
1 pint whipping cream
1 fluid ounce white chocolate liqueur
1 fluid ounce banana liqueur
12 ounces white chocolate
2 teaspoons unsweetened cocoa powder, for garnish

Directions

To Make White Chocolate Pastry Cream: In a medium bowl, whisk together egg yolks and sugar until pale yellow. Whisk in cornstarch. In a medium saucepan, heat milk and vanilla bean to just below the boiling point. Slowly whisk a small amount of hot milk into egg yolk mixture, then stir egg yolk mixture back into pan. Bring to a boil over low heat, stirring constantly.

Stir in butter, then strain mixture through a sieve. Place plastic wrap over the surface of mixture to keep a skin from forming. Allow to cool slightly, then stir in melted white chocolate. Chill pastry cream.

Slice bananas and toss with the lemon juice to keep from discoloring. Set aside.

In a large bowl, whip chilled whipping cream until stiff peaks form. Fold into pastry cream, then fold in bananas and liqueurs. Fill tart shell with banana cream filling.

Top generously with white chocolate curls, then dust with cocoa. Serve soon after assembling so crust doesn't get soggy.

To make white chocolate curls, carefully draw a vegetable peeler across the broad, flat surface of a room-temperature (about 80 degrees) chunk of white chocolate to make large, thin curls. Refrigerate until ready to use.

Poppy Seed and Banana Muffins

Ingredients

1 1/4 cups whole wheat flour
1 cup wheat bran
1/2 cup wheat germ
1 teaspoon baking soda
1 teaspoon baking powder
1/2 teaspoon salt (optional)
2 eggs
1/4 cup honey
1/4 cup vegetable oil
1 cup mashed bananas
1/2 cup milk
2 teaspoons lemon juice
1/3 cup poppy seeds

Directions

Preheat oven to 350 degrees F (175 degrees C). Lightly grease a 12 cup muffin pan.

In a large bowl, mix whole wheat flour, wheat bran, wheat germ, baking soda, baking powder, and salt.

In a medium bowl, beat together eggs, honey, and vegetable oil. Stir in bananas, milk, lemon juice, and poppy seeds.

Make a well in the center of the wheat flour mixture, and pour in egg and banana mixture. Stir until just blended. Spoon into the prepared muffin pan.

Bake 25 to 30 minutes in the preheated oven, until a toothpick inserted in the center comes out clean.

Banana Pound Cake With Caramel Glaze

Ingredients

3 cups all-purpose flour
1/2 teaspoon baking powder
1/2 teaspoon baking soda
1 teaspoon salt
1 cup butter
1/2 cup vegetable shortening
2 cups brown sugar
1 cup white sugar
4 ripe bananas, mashed
5 eggs
2 teaspoons vanilla extract
1/2 cup milk
1 cup chopped pecans

1/2 cup butter
1/4 cup brown sugar
1/4 cup white sugar
1 teaspoon vanilla extract
1/4 cup heavy cream

Directions

Preheat an oven to 325 degrees F (165 degrees C). Combine flour, baking powder, baking soda, and salt in a bowl. Set aside. Grease and flour a fluted tube pan.

Beat 1 cup of butter, shortening, 2 cups of brown sugar, and 1 cup of white sugar with an electric mixer in a large bowl until light and fluffy. The mixture should be noticeably lighter in color. Add the bananas, followed by the eggs one at a time, allowing each egg to blend into the butter mixture before adding the next. Beat in 2 teaspoons of vanilla extract with the last egg. Pour in the flour mixture alternately with the milk, mixing until just incorporated. Fold in the pecans; mixing just enough to evenly combine. Pour the batter into prepared pan.

Bake in the preheated oven until a toothpick inserted into the center comes out clean, about 1 hour and 20 minutes.

Meanwhile, prepare the glaze. Heat 1/2 cup of butter, 1/4 cup of brown sugar, 1/4 cup of white sugar, 1 teaspoon of vanilla extract, and heavy cream in a saucepan over medium heat. Stir continuously until the sugars have dissolved, then gently simmer for 1 minute. Pour over baked cake while still in the pan. Cool in the pan for 10 minutes before removing to cool completely on a wire rack.

Banana Oat Bars

Ingredients

1 1/3 cups quick cooking oats
1/2 cup white sugar
2 teaspoons baking powder
1 teaspoon ground cinnamon
1/2 teaspoon baking soda
1/2 cup raisins
1 cup mashed bananas
1/4 cup skim milk
2 egg whites
1 teaspoon vanilla extract

Directions

Preheat oven to 350 degrees F (175 degrees C).

Mix together dry ingredients. In a separate bowl mix together bananas, egg whites, milk and vanilla. Beat all together.

Bake in a 9 x 13 inch pan which has been sprayed with non-stick spray for about 35 minutes. Cool and cut into bars. You may sprinkle with cinnamon and sugar, if desired.

Banana and Black Bean Saute

Ingredients

1 tablespoon cooking oil
1 banana, chopped
2 tablespoons honey
3/4 (14.5 ounce) can black beans, rinsed and drained
1 tablespoon fresh lime juice
1 pinch salt
1 (14 ounce) can coconut milk

Directions

Heat the oil in a skillet over medium-high heat; cook the bananas in the hot oil until hot, 2 to 3 minutes. Stir the honey and black beans with the bananas; cook and stir another 2 to 3 minutes. Stir the lime juice and salt into the mixture. Pour the coconut milk over the mixture and stir. Allow the mixture to simmer until hot, about 5 minutes. Serve hot.

Maple Banana Bread

Ingredients

1/2 cup butter, melted
1/2 cup maple syrup
1 egg
2 ripe bananas
1/2 teaspoon maple extract
3 tablespoons milk
2 cups all-purpose flour
1 teaspoon baking soda 1/2
teaspoon baking powder 1/4
cup chopped walnuts
3 tablespoons white sugar

Directions

Preheat oven to 350 degrees F (175 degrees C). Grease a 5x9 inch loaf pan.

In a large bowl, mix the melted butter and maple syrup. Beat in the egg and bananas, leaving a few small chunks. Stir in the maple extract and milk. In a separate bowl, mix the flour, baking soda, and baking powder, and stir into the banana mixture just until moistened. Transfer to the prepared loaf pan. Mix the nuts and sugar, and sprinkle evenly over the batter.

Bake 50 minutes in the preheated oven, or until a knife inserted in the center of the loaf comes out clean.

Brown Sugar Banana Nut Bread I

Ingredients

1/2 cup butter, softened
1 cup brown sugar
2 eggs
1 tablespoon vanilla extract
4 very ripe bananas, mashed
2 cups all-purpose flour
3 teaspoons baking powder
1/2 teaspoon salt
1/2 cup chopped walnuts

Directions

Preheat oven to 350 degrees F (175 degrees C). Lightly grease a 9x5 inch loaf pan.

In a large bowl, cream together the butter and sugar until light and fluffy. Stir in the eggs one at a time, beating well with each addition. Stir in vanilla and banana. In a separate bowl, sift together flour, baking powder, and salt.

Blend the banana mixture into the flour mixture; stir just to combine. Fold in walnuts. Pour batter into prepared pan.

Bake in preheated oven for 1 hour, until a toothpick inserted into center of loaf comes out clean.

Banana Nut Yeast Bread

Ingredients

2 (.25 ounce) packages active dry yeast
1 1/3 cups warm water (110 degrees to 115 degrees)
1 cup mashed ripe bananas
1/2 cup sugar
1/3 cup warm milk (110 to 115 degrees F)
1/3 cup butter or margarine, softened
1/2 teaspoon salt
2 eggs
5 cups all-purpose flour
1/2 cup chopped nuts

Directions

In a mixing bowl, dissolve yeast in warm water. Add the bananas, sugar, milk, butter, salt, eggs and 3 cups flour. Beat on medium speed for 2 minutes. Stir in nuts. Stir in enough remaining flour to form a stiff batter. Do not knead. Spoon into two greased 9-in. x 5-in. x 3-in. loaf pans. Cover and let rise in a warm place until doubled, about 1-1/2 hours. Bake at 375 degrees F for 25-30 minutes or until a toothpick comes out clean. Remove from pans to wire racks to cool.

Samoan Green Banana

Ingredients

3 (13.5 ounce) cans coconut milk
1 large onion, chopped
6 small unripe (green) bananas

Directions

Combine the coconut milk and onion in a bowl; set aside.

Bring a large pot of water to a boil over medium heat. Boil the bananas in their skin for 30 to 40 minutes; drain. Run the bananas under cold water until they are cool enough to handle. Remove the bananas whole from their skins.

Heat a large saucepan over medium-high heat. Place the bananas in the pan. Pour the coconut milk mixture over the bananas. Cook until the coconut milk is foamy. Allow to cool 5 minutes before serving.

Janet's Famous Banana Nut Bread

Ingredients

3 cups white sugar
3/4 cup butter, softened
3 eggs
2 cups mashed ripe banana
1/2 cup sour cream
3 1/2 cups all-purpose flour
1 teaspoon baking soda
1/2 teaspoon baking powder
1/2 teaspoon ground cinnamon
1 1/2 cups chopped pecans

Directions

Preheat oven to 325 degrees F (165 degrees C). Lightly grease and flour two 8x4 inch pans.

In a large bowl, cream together the sugar and butter until light and fluffy. Stir in the eggs one at a time, beating well with each addition. Stir in the banana and sour cream.

In a separate bowl, combine the flour, baking soda, baking powder, cinnamon and pecans; stir into banana mixture, just until combined. Pour batter into prepared pans.

Bake in preheated oven for 55 to 65 minutes, until a toothpick inserted into center of a loaf comes out clean. Remove from pan and place on a wire rack to cool. Serve warm or cold.

Banana Bread

Ingredients

2/3 cup sugar
1/3 cup shortening
2 cups all-purpose flour
2 teaspoons baking powder
1/4 teaspoon baking soda
1/4 teaspoon salt
1 cup mashed ripe bananas

Directions

Note: This recipe does NOT contain eggs or milk. In a large bowl, cream sugar and shortening for about 5 minutes (mixture does not get smooth). Combine flour, baking powder, baking soda and salt; add to creamed mixture alternately with bananas, beating after each addition (the batter will be thick). Spoon into a greased 9-in. x 5-in. x 3-in. loaf pan. Bake at 350 degrees F for 40-45 minutes or until bread tests done with a toothpick. Cool in pan for 10 minutes before removing to a wire rack.

Banana Cake VII

Ingredients

1/2 cup butter, softened
1 cup white sugar
2 eggs
1 egg white
2 tablespoons milk
2 teaspoons vanilla extract
1 1/2 cups mashed bananas
1 1/2 cups all-purpose flour
1 1/4 teaspoons baking powder
1/2 teaspoon baking soda
1/2 teaspoon salt
1/4 teaspoon ground allspice

Directions

Preheat oven to 350 degrees F (175 degrees C). Sift flour, baking powder, soda, salt and allspice together and set aside.

In a large bowl, cream the butter and sugar until light and fluffy. Add eggs and egg white and beat well. Add the mashed banana, vanilla and milk. Add the flour mixture and mix until well blended.

Divide batter into two 9 inch pans. Bake at 350 degrees F (175 degrees C) for 25 to 30 minutes, or until a toothpick inserted into the center of the cake comes out clean. Cool completely and frost with Cream Cheese Frosting.

Banana Cake I

Ingredients

3 cups cake flour
1 teaspoon baking powder
1 1/8 teaspoons baking soda
3/4 cup unsalted butter
2 1/4 cups white sugar
3/4 teaspoon salt
3 eggs
1 1/2 cups mashed bananas
6 tablespoons buttermilk
1 teaspoon vanilla extract

Directions

Preheat oven to 375 degrees F (190 degrees C). Grease and flour 3, 9-inch round cake pans.

Sift the flour with the baking powder and soda.

In a large bowl, cream together the butter or margarine, sugar, and salt. Add eggs one at a time to the creamed mixture, beating well after each addition.

Add alternately to the creamed mixture the flour mixture, the bananas, and the buttermilk. Add vanilla, and mix well. Pour into the well greased pans.

Bake in a preheated 375 degrees F (190 degrees C) oven for 30 to 40 minutes. Let cake cool and frost with your choice of icings.

Banana Split Cheesecake

Ingredients

2 1/2 cups graham cracker crumbs
3/4 cup melted butter
4 cups confectioners' sugar
2 (8 ounce) packages cream cheese
1 (8 ounce) can crushed pineapple, drained
3 medium bananas, quartered
1 (12 ounce) container frozen whipped topping, thawed
8 maraschino cherries, halved
1/4 cup chocolate syrup
1/2 cup pecan halves

Directions

Blend the melted butter or margarine with the graham crackers and press into the bottom of one 9x12 inch pan.

Blend the confectioner's sugar and the cream cheese together until smooth. Spread over the graham cracker crumb layer. Layer the crushed pineapple and the bananas over the cream cheese layer. Then spread the whipped topping over the top. Decorate with maraschino cherry halves. Drizzle chocolate syrup over the top and sprinkle with pecans. Chill for at least 4 hours then serve.

Cathy's Banana Bread

Ingredients

1 cup mashed bananas
1 cup sour cream
1/4 cup margarine
1 1/3 cups white sugar
2 eggs
1 teaspoon vanilla extract
2 cups all-purpose flour
1 teaspoon baking soda
1 teaspoon baking powder
1/4 teaspoon salt

Directions

Preheat oven to 350 degrees F (175 degrees C). Grease and flour one 9x13 inch pan, or two 7x3 inch loaf pans.

Combine banana and sour cream. Set aside. In a large bowl, cream together the margarine and sugar until smooth. Beat in the eggs one at a time, then stir in the vanilla and banana mixture. Combine the flour, baking soda, baking powder and salt; stir into the banana mixture. Spread the batter evenly into the prepared pan or pans.

Bake for 50 minutes in the preheated oven, or until a toothpick inserted into the center of the bread comes out clean.

Chocolate Chip Banana Bread II

Ingredients

1 cup shortening
2 cups white sugar
2 eggs
2 tablespoons mayonnaise
6 very ripe bananas, mashed
3 cups all-purpose flour
1/2 teaspoon salt
1 teaspoon baking powder
2 teaspoons baking soda
1 cup semi-sweet chocolate chips
1/2 cup chopped walnuts

Directions

Preheat oven to 350 degrees F (175 degrees C). Lightly grease two 9x5 inch loaf pans.

In a large bowl, cream together the shortening and sugar until light and fluffy. Stir in the eggs one at a time, beating well with each addition. Stir in the mayonnaise and bananas. Stir together the flour, salt, baking powder and baking soda. Blend the flour mixture into the banana mixture; stir just enough to evenly combine. Fold in the chocolate chips and walnuts.

Bake at 350 degrees F (175 degrees C) until a toothpick inserted into the center of the loaf comes out clean, about 50 to 75 minutes. Cool loaf in the pan for 20 minutes before removing to a wire rack to cool completely.

Stovetop Banana Pudding

Ingredients

2 eggs
1 1/2 cups milk
1 pinch salt
1 tablespoon vanilla extract
3/4 cup all-purpose flour
6 bananas, peeled and sliced
1 (16 ounce) package vanilla wafer cookies
1 pinch ground nutmeg
1 pinch ground cinnamon

Directions

In large pot, combine eggs, milk, salt, vanilla, and flour. Stir over low heat until mixture boils and thickens. Remove from heat and stir in bananas and cookies. Top with nutmeg and cinnamon to taste. Serve.

Strawberry Banana Torte

Ingredients

1 (10 inch) prepared angel food cake
2 cups heavy cream
1/2 teaspoon cornstarch
3 pints strawberries
1/2 cup white sugar
1 cup sour cream
1 dash red food coloring (optional)
3 bananas, sliced

Directions

Slice the angel food cake horizontally into 3 layers using a long serrated knife.

Whip cream with cornstarch in a large bowl until stiff, but not grainy. In a separate bowl, crush about 1/2 cup of the strawberries. Stir in sugar and sour cream. Mix in red food coloring if desired. Gently fold the strawberry mixture into the whipped cream. Refrigerate until ready to use.

Set aside 6 or 8 nice looking whole strawberries to use for garnish. Remove stems from remaining berries, and slice.

Place the bottom slice of angel food cake onto a serving plate. Top with a layer of sliced strawberries and bananas. Spread a layer of the whipped cream over the fruit. Top with the center layer of the cake, and repeat the fruit and cream layers. Place the top layer of the cake on top. Frost the top and sides of the cake with the remaining whipped cream mixture. Arrange whole strawberries on top for garnish. Refrigerate until serving.

Banana Split Pie

Ingredients

1/2 cup butter
1 1/2 cups confectioners' sugar
2 eggs
1 teaspoon vanilla extract
2 bananas
1 tablespoon lemon juice
1 (1 ounce) square unsweetened chocolate, grated
1 (9 inch) pie crust, baked

Directions

Cream together butter or margarine and confectioner's sugar. Beat in eggs one at a time; beat for 3 minutes after each addition. Stir in vanilla.

Slice 2 bananas, and sprinkle with lemon juice. Fold grated chocolate and bananas into sugar mixture. Turn filling into cooled pie shell. Garnish with walnuts, banana slices, and whipped cream.

For more information regarding egg safety, read our Hints and Tips.

Banana-Zucchini Bread

Ingredients

3 eggs
3/4 cup vegetable oil
2/3 cup packed brown sugar
1 cup white sugar
1 cup grated zucchini
2 bananas, mashed
2 teaspoons vanilla extract
3 1/2 cups all-purpose flour
1 tablespoon ground cinnamon
1 1/2 teaspoons baking powder
1 teaspoon baking soda
1 teaspoon salt
1/2 cup dried cranberries
1/2 cup chopped walnuts

Directions

Preheat oven to 325 degrees F (165 degrees C). Grease and flour two 8x4 inch bread loaf pans.

In a large bowl, beat eggs until light yellow and frothy. Add oil, brown sugar, white sugar, grated zucchini, bananas, and vanilla; blend together until well combined. Stir in the flour, cinnamon, baking powder, baking soda, and salt. Mix in the cranberries and nuts. Divide the batter evenly between the two prepared loaf pans.

Bake in the preheated oven until a toothpick inserted in the center comes out clean, about 50 minutes. Allow to cool in the loaf pans on a wire rack before removing and serving.

Banana Snack Cake

Ingredients

1 cup white sugar
1 cup butter
2 eggs
1/2 cup buttermilk
1 cup mashed bananas
1 teaspoon vanilla extract
2 cups all-purpose flour
1 cup quick cooking oats
1 1/2 teaspoons baking soda
1 teaspoon salt
1/2 cup chopped walnuts
1/2 cup flaked coconut
2 cups semisweet chocolate chips

Directions

Preheat oven to 350 degrees F (175 degrees C). Grease and flour a 9x13 inch pan. In a medium bowl, mix flour, oats, baking soda and salt together and set aside.

In a large bowl, cream butter and sugar until light and fluffy. Add eggs one at a time, mixing well with each addition. Mix in buttermilk, bananas and vanilla. Add flour mixture and mix well. Finally, fold in the nuts, coconut and 1 cup of the chocolate chips.

Pour batter into a 9x13 inch pan. Sprinkle top with remaining 1 cup of chocolate chips. Bake at 350 degrees F (175 degrees C) for 30 to 35 minutes, or until a toothpick inserted into the cake comes out clean.

Banana Chip Muffins II

Ingredients

1 1/2 cups all-purpose flour
1 1/4 teaspoons baking powder
1/2 teaspoon baking soda
1/2 teaspoon ground cinnamon
1/8 teaspoon salt
2 egg whites
1 cup mashed bananas
3/4 cup white sugar
1/4 cup applesauce
1/2 cup semisweet chocolate chips

Directions

Preheat oven to 400 degrees F (205 degrees C). Coat a 12 cup muffin tin with nonstick spray.

Whisk together flour, baking powder, soda, cinnamon, salt, and sugar. Mix in egg whites, applesauce, and banana mash until just moistened. Stir in chocolate chips. Divide batter into muffin cups.

Bake for 15 to 18 minutes.

Banana Split Bread

Ingredients

1/2 cup butter or margarine, softened
1 cup sugar
1 egg
1 cup mashed ripe bananas
3 tablespoons milk
2 cups all-purpose flour
1 teaspoon baking powder
1/2 teaspoon baking soda
1 cup semisweet chocolate chips
1/2 cup chopped pecans

Directions

In a mixing bowl, cream butter and sugar. beat in egg. In a small bowl, combine bananas and milk. Combine the flour, baking powder and baking soda; add to creamed mixture alternately with banana mixture. Fold in chocolate chips and pecans.

Pour into a greased 9-in. x 5-in. x 3-in. loaf pan. Bake at 350 degrees F for 60-70 minutes or until a toothpick inserted near the center comes out clean. Cool for 10 minutes before removing from pan to a wire rack.

Hot Banana Salsa

Ingredients

1 large firm banana, peeled and diced
1/2 cup red bell pepper, seeded and diced
1/2 cup green bell pepper, seeded and diced
1/2 cup yellow bell pepper, seeded and diced
3 tablespoons chopped fresh cilantro
2 green onions, chopped
2 tablespoons fresh lime juice
1 tablespoon brown sugar
2 teaspoons minced fresh ginger root
2 teaspoons olive oil
1 teaspoon minced habanero pepper
salt to taste

Directions

Mix together the banana, red pepper, green pepper, yellow pepper, cilantro, green onion, lime juice, brown sugar, ginger, olive oil, and habanero pepper in a bowl; season with salt. Serve within 1 hour.

Pineapple Banana Bread

Ingredients

3 cups all-purpose flour
2 cups sugar
1 teaspoon salt
1 teaspoon baking soda
1 teaspoon ground cinnamon
3 eggs
1 1/4 cups vegetable oil
2 teaspoons vanilla extract
1 (8 ounce) can crushed pineapple, drained
2 cups mashed ripe bananas

Directions

In a large bowl, combine the flour, sugar, salt, baking soda and cinnamon. In another bowl, beat the eggs, oil and vanilla; add pineapple and bananas. Stir into the dry ingredients just until moistened. Pour into two greased 8-in. x 4-in. x 2-in. loaf pans.

Bake at 350 degrees F for 60-65 minutes or until a toothpick comes out clean. Cool for 10 minutes before removing from pans to wire racks.

Oatmeal Banana Nut Cookies

Ingredients

1 cup butter
1 cup white sugar
1 cup packed brown sugar
2 eggs
1 teaspoon banana extract
1 1/2 cups all-purpose flour
1 teaspoon baking soda
1/2 teaspoon salt
3 cups rolled oats
2 cups chopped pecans

Directions

Preheat oven to 375 degrees F (190 degrees C).

Cream butter or margarine with mixer. Blend in whole eggs, sugar, and extract. Add flour, baking soda, and salt. When the ingredients are thoroughly mixed, add oats and pecans. Mix on lower speed until consistent.

Drop pieces of the dough using an ice cream scoop onto an ungreased cookie tray roughly 3 to 4 inches apart.

Bake 8 to 10 minutes. Eight minutes would yield crispy cookies with a chewy, slightly doughy center. For harder, crispier cookies, bake longer. Cool on wire rack.

Honey-Baked Bananas

Ingredients

2 medium firm bananas. sliced
1 tablespoon butter or margarine, melted
2 teaspoons honey
1/2 teaspoon lemon juice
1/4 cup flaked coconut, toasted
1/4 cup chopped pecans, toasted
whipped topping

Directions

Place the bananas in a greased 1-qt. baking dish. Combine the butter, honey and lemon juice; drizzle over bananas. Bake, uncovered, at 350 degrees F for 10-12 minutes or until heated through. Sprinkle each serving with coconut and pecans; top with a dollop of whipped topping.

The Anna Banana

Ingredients

1/4 cup banana liqueur
2 tablespoons coconut rum
2 tablespoons peach schnapps
1 1/2 cups vanilla ice cream
1 teaspoon vanilla extract

Directions

In the container of a blender, combine the banana liqueur, coconut rum, peach schnapps, vanilla ice cream and vanilla extract. Cover and blend until smooth. Serve in coconuts for fun!

Banana Nut Cupcakes

Ingredients

1/3 cup butter flavored shortening
2/3 cup sugar
1 cup mashed ripe bananas
2 eggs
2 tablespoons milk
1 tablespoon vanilla extract
1 1/3 cups all-purpose flour
2 teaspoons baking powder
1/2 teaspoon baking soda
1/4 teaspoon salt
1/4 cup chopped nuts

Directions

In a mixing bowl, cream shortening and sugar. Beat in the bananas, eggs, milk and vanilla. Combine the flour, baking powder, baking soda and salt; gradually add to creamed mixture until combined. Stir in nuts.

Fill paper-lined muffin cups two-thirds full. Bake at 350 degrees F for 18-20 minutes or until a toothpick comes out clean. Cool for 5 minutes before removing from pans to wire racks.

Curried Banana Sauce

Ingredients

1/2 teaspoon olive oil
2 small ripe bananas, quartered
1 shallot, quartered
1 clove garlic, halved
1/4 cup chopped sweet onion (such as Vidalia®)
1 3/4 teaspoons curry powder, or to taste
3/4 cup low-sodium chicken broth
1 tablespoon rice vinegar
1 1/2 teaspoons honey
1 pinch salt

Directions

Heat the olive oil in a skillet over medium heat. Stir in the bananas, shallot, garlic, and onion. Cook and stir until the onion has softened and turned translucent, about 5 minutes. Stir in curry powder and cook until fragrant, about 30 seconds. Pour in the chicken chicken broth and simmer for about 5 minutes, stirring occasionally.

Pour the curry mixture, rice vinegar, honey, and salt into a blender, filling the pitcher no more than halfway full. Hold down the lid of the blender with a folded kitchen towel, and carefully start the blender, using a few quick pulses to get the curry moving before leaving it on to puree. Puree in batches until smooth and pour into a clean pot. Alternately, you can use a stick blender and puree the curry right in the cooking pot.

Banana Pancake Muffins

Ingredients

1/2 cup shortening
1 cup brown sugar
1 egg
1 banana, diced
3 cups all-purpose flour
1 1/2 teaspoons baking powder
1/2 teaspoon baking soda
1 1/4 cups soy milk

Directions

Preheat oven to 350 degrees F (175 degrees C). Grease 12 muffin cups or line with paper muffin liners.

In a large bowl, cream together shortening and sugar. Beat in egg. Blend until banana is completely mixed in, then add flour, baking powder and baking soda. Mix batter with spoon. Stir in soy milk, then spoon into muffin pan. Spoon batter into prepared muffin cups.

Bake in preheated oven for 15 to 20 minutes, until a toothpick inserted into center of muffin comes out clean.

Chilled Banana and Coconut Soup

Ingredients

2 pounds bananas, peeled and diced
1 lemon, juiced
1/2 cup pineapple juice
1 cup plain yogurt
1 cup vanilla ice cream
1/4 cup dark rum
2 cups canned coconut milk
1/4 cup sliced almonds, toasted

Directions

In a large bowl, combine the bananas, lemon juice, pineapple juice, yogurt, ice cream, rum and coconut milk. Ladle into a blender in batches if necessary, and blend until smooth. Refrigerate until chilled.

Divide the cold soup among chilled serving bowls, and sprinkle sliced almonds over the top for garnish.

Banana Nut Bread

Ingredients

1 (18.25 ounce) package yellow
cake mix
1 egg
1/2 cup milk
1 cup mashed ripe bananas
1/2 cup chopped pecans

Directions

In a mixing bowl, combine cake mix, egg and milk. Add bananas; beat on medium speed for 2 minutes. Stir in pecans. Pour into two greased 8-in. x 4-in. x 2-in. loaf pans. Bake at 350 degrees F for 40 -45 minutes or until a toothpick inserted near the center comes out clean. Cool for 10 minutes before removing from pans to wire racks to cool completely.

Raisin Banana Bread

Ingredients

3 cups all-purpose flour
2 cups sugar
1 teaspoon baking powder
1 teaspoon salt
1 teaspoon pumpkin pie spice
1/2 teaspoon baking soda
1/2 teaspoon ground cinnamon
3 eggs
1 cup vegetable oil
2 teaspoons vanilla extract
1 cup grated zucchini
1 cup grated carrot
1/2 cup mashed ripe banana
1/2 cup raisins
1/2 cup chopped walnuts

Directions

In a mixing bowl, combine the first seven ingredients. Add eggs, oil and vanilla; mix well. Stir in zucchini, carrot, banana, raisins and nuts. Pour into four greased and floured 5-3/4-in. x 3-in. x 2-in. loaf pans. Bake at 350 degrees F for 45-48 minutes or until a toothpick inserted near the center comes out clean. Cool for 10 minutes; remove from pans to wire racks.

Apple Banana Cupcakes

Ingredients

2 cups all-purpose flour
1 teaspoon baking soda
1 teaspoon salt
1/2 teaspoon ground cinnamon
1/2 teaspoon ground nutmeg 2/3 cup shortening
1 1/4 cups white sugar
2 eggs
1 teaspoon vanilla extract
1/4 cup buttermilk
1 cup ripe bananas, mashed
2 apples - peeled, cored and shredded

Directions

Preheat oven to 375 degrees F (190 degrees C). Grease and flour 24 muffin cups, or use paper liners. Sift together the flour, baking soda, salt, cinnamon, and nutmeg. Set aside.

In a large bowl, cream together the shortening and sugar until light and fluffy. Beat in the eggs one at a time, then stir in the vanilla and buttermilk. Beat in the flour mixture, mixing just until incorporated. Fold in the mashed bananas and shredded apples. Fill each muffin cup half full.

Bake in the preheated oven for 20 to 25 minutes, or until a toothpick inserted into the center comes out clean. Allow to cool.

Banana Sour Cream Bread

Ingredients

1/4 cup white sugar
1 teaspoon ground cinnamon
3/4 cup butter
3 cups white sugar
3 eggs
6 very ripe bananas, mashed
1 (16 ounce) container sour cream
2 teaspoons vanilla extract
2 teaspoons ground cinnamon
1/2 teaspoon salt
3 teaspoons baking soda
4 1/2 cups all-purpose flour
1 cup chopped walnuts (optional)

Directions

Preheat oven to 300 degrees F (150 degrees C). Grease four 7x3 inch loaf pans. In a small bowl, stir together 1/4 cup white sugar and 1 teaspoon cinnamon. Dust pans lightly with cinnamon and sugar mixture.

In a large bowl, cream butter and 3 cups sugar. Mix in eggs, mashed bananas, sour cream, vanilla and cinnamon. Mix in salt, baking soda and flour. Stir in nuts. Divide into prepared pans.

Bake for 1 hour, until a toothpick inserted in center comes out clean.

Banana Split Pudding

Ingredients

2/3 cup sugar
2 tablespoons Argo® Corn Starch
1/4 teaspoon salt
2 cups milk
2 egg yolks
2 tablespoons butter
1 teaspoon Spice Islands® Pure Vanilla Extract
2 bananas, sliced
1/4 cup fudge topping

Directions

Mix sugar, corn starch and salt in a large microwaveable bowl. Whisk in milk and egg yolks until well blended.

Microwave on HIGH (100%) for about 5 to 7 minutes, stirring every 1 to 2 minutes. Cook until pudding is thick and has boiled at least 1 minute. Remove from microwave. Stir in butter and vanilla. Cover surface with plastic wrap.

Chill 30 minutes.

Layer pudding with bananas and fudge topping in individual clear serving bowls. Garnish with whipped topping, chopped pecans and cherries, if desired.

Banana Cream Dessert

Ingredients

4 medium firm bananas, sliced
1/2 cup lemon juice
1 1/2 cups graham cracker crumbs
1/4 cup sugar
1/2 cup butter or margarine, melted
1 cup sour cream
1 (3.4 ounce) package instant vanilla pudding mix
1 (12 ounce) container frozen whipped topping, thawed
1/3 cup chopped pecans

Directions

Toss bananas with lemon juice; drain well and set aside. In a bowl, combine the cracker crumbs, sugar and butter. Press into a greased 9-in. springform pan.

In a small mixing bowl, beat the sour cream and pudding mix on low speed for 2 minutes. Fold in banana and whipped topping. Pour into prepared crust. Chill for up to 6 hours. Sprinkle with pecans.

Banana Smoothie I

Ingredients

1 banana
1 cup milk
1 teaspoon vanilla extract
1 egg
2 tablespoons white sugar
1 pinch ground cinnamon

Directions

In a blender, combine banana, milk, vanilla, egg and sugar. Blend until smooth. Pour into a tall glass and top with a pinch of cinnamon.

Banana Honey Yogurt Ice

Ingredients

4 bananas, sliced
1 1/4 cups Greek yogurt
1 tablespoon lemon juice
2 tablespoons honey
1/2 teaspoon ground cinnamon

Directions

Place bananas, yogurt, lemon juice, honey, and cinnamon into a blender. Puree until smooth, then pour into a freezer-safe container. Freeze until nearly solid, then scrape back into blender, and puree again until smooth. Return to freezer, and freeze until solid.

Banana Muffins I

Ingredients

1 cup all-purpose flour
1 tablespoon baking powder
1/2 teaspoon baking soda 1/4 teaspoon salt
1 cup mashed ripe banana
1/4 cup white sugar
1/4 cup sour cream
1 egg
1/2 teaspoon vanilla extract

Directions

Preheat oven to 350 degrees F (175 degrees C). Grease muffin cups or line with paper muffin liners.

Mix together flour, baking powder, baking soda and salt. In a separate bowl, beat together banana, sugar, egg and vanilla. Stir in the sour cream. Stir banana mixture into flour until just combined. Scoop batter into prepared muffin cups.

Bake in preheated oven for 15 to 20 minutes, or until a toothpick inserted into center of a muffin comes out clean. Let cool before serving. For best flavor, place in an airtight container or bag overnight.

Special Banana Bread

Ingredients

1 cup shortening
2 cups white sugar
6 very ripe bananas, mashed
4 eggs
2 1/4 cups all-purpose flour
1 teaspoon salt
2 teaspoons baking soda
2 teaspoons ground cinnamon
1 teaspoon ground cloves
1 teaspoon freshly grated nutmeg
1 cup chopped walnuts

Directions

Preheat oven to 350 degrees F (175 degrees C). Spray two 9x5 inch loaf pans with non-stick cooking spray.

Cream the shortening and sugar until light. Beat in the eggs one at a time.

Sift together the flour, salt, baking soda, cinnamon, cloves, and nutmeg. Add to the shortening mixture and mix to combine.

Thoroughly mash the bananas. Stir bananas into the batter then stir in the walnuts. Pour the batter into the prepared pans.

Bake at 350 degrees F (175 degrees C) for 45 minutes to 1 hour or until a wooden skewer inserted near the center comes out clean. Check with a wooden skewer every 15 minutes after 45 minutes of baking. It can take up to 65 to 70 minutes to cook.

Grandma's Homemade Banana Bread

Ingredients

1 1/2 cups white sugar
1/2 cup butter, softened
3 bananas, mashed
2 eggs
2 cups all-purpose flour 1/2
teaspoon baking soda 1/3
cup sour milk
1/4 teaspoon salt
1 teaspoon vanilla extract

Directions

Preheat oven to 350 degrees F (175 degrees C). Lightly grease an 8x4 inch loaf pan.

Combine sugar, butter, bananas, eggs, flour, baking soda, milk, salt and vanilla extract in a large mixing bowl; beat well. Pour batter into prepared pan.

Bake in a preheated oven for 60 minutes, or until a toothpick inserted into the center of the loaf comes out clean.

Banana Milk Drink

Ingredients

1 large ripe banana
1 cup milk
1 1/2 teaspoons sugar
1/2 teaspoon vanilla extract
1 dash ground cinnamon

Directions

Place the first four ingredients in a blender; cover and process until smooth. Pour into glasses; sprinkle with cinnamon if desired. Serve immediately.

Cardamom Banana Bread

Ingredients

2/3 cup raisins
1/3 cup dark rum
3 ripe bananas, mashed 3/4
cup packed brown sugar 1/3
cup canola oil
2 eggs
1 cup all-purpose flour
3/4 cup whole wheat flour
1 teaspoon baking powder
1 teaspoon baking soda
1 teaspoon salt
1 teaspoon ground cardamom
1/2 cup chopped walnuts, toasted

Directions

Preheat oven to 350 degrees F (175 degrees C). Grease one 9x5 inch loaf pan.

In a small saucepan, combine the raisins and the rum. Cook over medium heat until simmering, then remove from the heat and allow to cool 10 minutes.

In a large bowl, mix together the mashed bananas, brown sugar, canola oil, and eggs with an electric mixer for 1 minute. Sift together the all-purpose flour, whole wheat flour, baking powder, baking soda, salt, and ground cardamom; stir into the egg mixture with a spoon until well blended, Stir in the walnuts and the rum soaked raisins last. Pour the batter into the prepared pan.

Bake in the preheated oven for 50 to 60 minutes, or until a toothpick inserted comes out clean. Allow bread to cool slightly before removing from the pan.

Cambodian Tapioca-Banana Pudding

Ingredients

1/2 cup small pearl tapioca
7 cups water, divided
5 medium ripe bananas, sliced
1/4 teaspoon salt
1/2 cup white sugar
3/4 cup coconut milk

Directions

Place 2 cups of water in a microwave-safe dish and heat until warm in the microwave, about 2 minutes. Add the tapioca and let stand for 10 minutes. Drain in a sieve. You'll have a mushy puddle of tapioca left over.

Pour the remaining water into a saucepan and add the drained tapioca. Bring to a boil, then simmer over medium heat until the tapioca begins to turn transparent. Stir frequently to avoid sticking.

When the tapioca is transparent, stir in the bananas, sugar and salt. Simmer for 10 to 15 more minutes, stirring frequently. When the bananas are broken down fairly well, remove from the heat and stir in the coconut milk until well blended. The tapioca pearls will become visible and the pudding will be the consistency of thick soup. Taste and adjust the sugar if desired.

Cool to room temperature or slightly warmer. Stir again before serving.

Chocolate Strawberry Banana Milkshake

Ingredients

1 cup low-fat milk
1/2 cup frozen unsweetened strawberries
1/2 ripe banana
2 tablespoons powdered chocolate drink mix
1/2 teaspoon vanilla extract
2 teaspoons white sugar

Directions

In a blender combine milk, frozen strawberries, 1/2 banana, chocolate milk powder, vanilla and sugar. Blend until smooth. If consistency is too runny, you may add more strawberries.

Cherry Banana Mini Loaves

Ingredients

1/2 cup butter or margarine, softened
1 cup sugar
2 eggs
1 cup mashed bananas
2 cups all-purpose flour
1 teaspoon baking soda
1/4 cup chopped walnuts
1/4 cup miniature semisweet chocolate chips
1/4 cup dried cherries or cranberries

Directions

In a mixing bowl, cream butter and sugar. Add eggs and banana; mix well. Combine flour and baking soda; gradually add to the creamed mixture. Fold in the nuts, chips and cherries. Transfer to four greased 5-3/4-in. x 3-in. x 2-in. loaf pans. Bake at 350 degrees F for 32-37 minutes or until a toothpick inserted near the center comes out clean. Cool for 10 minutes before removing from pans to wire racks.

Banana-Nut Bundt Cake

Ingredients

3 cups all-purpose flour
2 cups sugar
1 teaspoon baking soda
1 teaspoon ground cinnamon
3 eggs, beaten
1 cup vegetable oil
2 cups finely chopped ripe bananas
1 (8 ounce) can crushed pineapple, undrained
1 1/2 teaspoons vanilla extract
1/2 cup flaked coconut
1 cup chopped nuts

Directions

In a large bowl, combine the flour, sugar, baking soda and cinnamon. In another bowl, combine the eggs, oil, bananas, pineapple and vanilla; stir into dry ingredients just until combined. Fold in coconut and nuts. Pour into a greased 10-in. fluted tube pan.

Bake at 350 degrees F for 60-70 minutes or until a toothpick inserted near the center comes out clean. Cool for 10 minutes before removing cake from pan to a wire rack to cool completely.

Extreme Banana Nut Bread 'EBNB'

Ingredients

2 cups all-purpose flour
1 teaspoon salt
2 teaspoons baking soda
1 cup butter or margarine
2 cups white sugar
2 cups mashed overripe bananas
4 eggs, beaten
1 cup chopped walnuts

Directions

Preheat the oven to 350 degrees F (175 degrees C). Grease and flour two 9x5 inch loaf pans.

Sift the flour, salt and baking soda into a large bowl. In a separate bowl, mix together the butter or margarine and sugar until smooth. Stir in the bananas, eggs, and walnuts until well blended. Pour the wet ingredients into the dry mixture, and stir just until blended. Divide the batter evenly between the two loaf pans.

Bake for 60 to 70 minutes in the preheated oven, until a knife inserted into the crown of the loaf comes out clean. Let the loaves cool in the pans for at least 5 minutes, then turn out onto a cooling rack, and cool completely. Wrap in aluminum foil to keep in the moisture. Ideally, refrigerate the loaves for 2 hours or more before serving.

Banana and Peanut Butter Pancakes

Ingredients

1 cup all-purpose flour
1 1/4 teaspoons baking powder
1 teaspoon brown sugar
1/4 teaspoon salt
1/4 cup creamy peanut butter
1 1/2 cups milk
1/4 teaspoon vanilla extract
1 small banana, peeled and chopped

Directions

Combine flour, baking powder, brown sugar, and salt in a large bowl. Mix in the peanut butter until the texture resembles cornmeal. Add milk and vanilla; stir just until blended. Stir in the banana pieces.

Heat a large skillet over medium heat, and coat with cooking spray. Spoon batter onto the skillet, using approximately 2 tablespoons to form each silver dollar pancake. Cook until pancakes are golden brown on both sides; serve hot.

Banana Pineapple Delight

Ingredients

2 cups crushed graham crackers
1/2 cup margarine, melted
1/2 cup margarine
2 cups confectioners' sugar
2 eggs
4 tablespoons cornstarch
1 tablespoon vanilla extract
3 bananas
1/4 cup lemon juice
1 (20 ounce) can crushed pineapple in heavy syrup, drained
1 (8 ounce) container frozen whipped topping, thawed

Directions

Combine graham cracker crumbs and melted margarine, and pat into bottom of 9x13-inch pan.

In medium, non-stick saucepan over medium heat, combine remaining margarine, confectioners' sugar, eggs, corn starch and vanilla. Bring to a boil, stirring frequently. Continue stirring, reduce heat and simmer 8 to 10 minutes. Let cool, then spread over crust.

Peel and slice bananas, dipping each piece in lemon juice to prevent browning, and layer over custard mixture. Layer pineapple on top of bananas. Cover all with whipped topping. Keep refrigerated until serving.

Banana Cream Pie IV

Ingredients

1 (9 inch) prepared graham cracker crust
1 large banana, sliced
2 cups cold milk
2 (3.5 ounce) packages instant vanilla pudding mix
1/2 teaspoon ground cinnamon
1 (8 ounce) container frozen whipped topping, thawed
1/4 cup caramel ice cream topping

Directions

Place banana slices in bottom of pie crust.

In a large bowl, combine milk, pudding mixes and cinnamon. Beat with wire whisk for 1 minute.

Gently stir in whipped topping to pudding, then spoon mixture into pie crust.

Cover and refrigerate for 4 hours until pie is set up. When pie is ready serve with caramel topping.

Strawberry-Banana French Toast

Ingredients

10 day-old French bread
5 eggs, lightly beaten
3/4 cup milk
1 tablespoon vanilla extract
1/4 teaspoon baking powder
1 (16 ounce) package frozen sweetened whole strawberries
4 firm bananas, sliced
1 cup sugar
1 tablespoon pumpkin pie or apple pie spice
1 tablespoon cinnamon sugar

Directions

Place bread slices in a large shallow baking dish. Combine eggs, milk, vanilla and baking powder; pour over bread. Cover and chill 8 hours or overnight. Remove from refrigerator 30 minutes before baking. In a bowl, combine strawberries, bananas, sugar and pie spice; pour into a greased 13-in. x 9-in. x 2-in. baking dish. Arrange prepared bread on top. Sprinkle with cinnamon sugar. Bake, uncovered, at 400 degrees F for 30-35 minutes.

Bellyful of Barbecued Bananas

Ingredients

4 bananas
1 tablespoon lemon juice
1 cup brown sugar
1 teaspoon ground cinnamon
2 cups vanilla ice cream

Directions

Preheat grill for low heat.

Halve each of the bananas lengthwise, then widthwise. Sprinkle bananas with lemon juice. In a small bowl, mix together the brown sugar and cinnamon. Roll banana pieces in sugar/cinnamon mixture until well coated.

Lightly oil the grill grate. Arrange bananas on preheated grill, and cook for 3 minutes per side. Serve in a bowl with vanilla ice cream topped with a sprinkling of remaining cinnamon/sugar mixture. Yum!

Bittersweet Banana Pudding

Ingredients

1 (16 ounce) package silken tofu
2 cups semi-sweet chocolate chips
2 ripe bananas
2 tablespoons raspberry vinegar

Directions

Blend tofu and bananas in a blender.

Melt chocolate in a double boiler.

Pour the chocolate into the blender, blend well. Add the vinegar to the blender. Mix until all of the ingredients are combined. Pour mixture into a shallow dish. Refrigerate for three hours.

Oatmeal Banana Cupcakes

Ingredients

1/2 cup butter or margarine, softened
1/2 cup sugar
2 eggs
1 cup mashed ripe bananas
3/4 cup honey
1 1/2 cups all-purpose flour
1 cup quick-cooking oats
1 teaspoon baking powder
1 teaspoon baking soda
3/4 teaspoon salt

Directions

In a mixing bowl, cream butter and sugar. Add eggs, bananas and honey; mix well. Combine dry ingredients; stir into creamed mixture just until moistened. Fill paper-lined muffin cups two-thirds full. Bake at 350 degrees F for 18-20 minutes or until cupcakes test done. Cool in pan 10 minutes before removing to a wire rack.

Banana Walnut Cake

Ingredients

1 (18.25 ounce) package banana cake mix
3/4 teaspoon baking powder
3 medium bananas
3 eggs
1/2 cup water
1/3 cup vegetable oil
1 1/2 cups chopped walnuts
CRUMB TOPPING:
1/2 cup sugar
1/2 cup all-purpose flour
1/4 cup butter

Directions

Place first seven ingredients in a large mixing bowl. Beat on low speed just until combined, then on medium for 2 minutes. Pour into a greased and floured 10-in. tube pan or a 13-in. x 9-in. x 2-in. baking pan. In a small bowl, combine topping ingredients until crumbly; sprinkle evenly over batter. Bake at 350 degrees F for 45 minutes. Cool. Store well-wrapped in refrigerator.

Chocolate Banana Smoothie

Ingredients

1 banana
1 tablespoon chocolate syrup
1 cup milk
1 cup crushed ice

Directions

In a blender, combine banana, chocolate syrup, milk and crushed ice. Blend until smooth. Pour into glasses and serve.

Banana Pudding II

Ingredients

2 eggs, beaten
2 1/2 cups milk
1/2 cup white sugar
2 tablespoons cornstarch
1/4 teaspoon salt
1 teaspoon vanilla extract
1 tablespoon margarine
32 vanilla wafers
4 bananas, sliced

Directions

In a double boiler over simmering water, combine eggs, milk, sugar, cornstarch and salt. Stir constantly and cook until thick, 10 to 15 minutes. Remove from heat and stir in vanilla and margarine.

Place a layer of 16 wafers in a glass serving dish. Top with half the bananas. Top with half the pudding. Repeat. Serve immediately or refrigerate until serving.

Banana-Nut Corn Bread

Ingredients

2 (8.5 ounce) packages corn bread/muffin mix
1 cup mashed ripe bananas
1 cup chopped walnuts
1 cup milk

Directions

In a bowl, combine all ingredients just until blended. Spoon into two greased 8-in. x 4-in. x 2-in. loaf pans. Bake at 350 degrees F for 35 -40 minutes or until a toothpick inserted near the center comes out clean. Cool for 10 minutes before removing from pans to wire racks to cool completely.

Spiced Banana Bread

Ingredients

2 cups flour
1 1/2 teaspoons baking powder
1 teaspoon baking soda
4 very ripe bananas
2 eggs
1 cup sugar
1 teaspoon cinnamon
1/2 teaspoon salt
1/2 teaspoon nutmeg
1/4 teaspoon ground cloves
1/2 cup melted butter
1 teaspoon vanilla extract

Directions

Preheat oven to 350 degrees F (175 degrees C). Grease and flour two 8x3 inch loaf pans. Whisk together the flour, baking powder, and baking soda; set aside.

Mash the bananas, eggs, sugar, cinnamon, salt, nutmeg, and cloves together in a large bowl with a fork until well combined. Stir in the melted butter and vanilla extract, then fold in the flour mixture until a batter forms and no dry lumps remain. Pour into the prepared loaf pans.

Bake in preheated oven until a toothpick inserted into the center comes out clean, about 45 minutes. Cool in the pan for 10 minutes, then remove from the pan, and allow to cool completely on a wire rack.

Orange Banana Salad

Ingredients

1 medium navel orange, sectioned
2 tablespoons flaked coconut, toasted
2 tablespoons orange juice
1/8 teaspoon ground cinnamon
1 medium ripe banana, sliced

Directions

Cut orange sections into bite-size pieces. In a bowl, combine the orange, coconut, orange juice and cinnamon if desired; toss gently. Refrigerate until chilled. Just before serving, add banana and toss gently.

Blueberry Banana Bread

Ingredients

2 cups all-purpose flour
1 teaspoon baking soda
1/2 teaspoon salt
1/2 cup shortening
1 cup sugar
2 eggs
2 teaspoons vanilla extract
2 medium ripe bananas, mashed
1 cup fresh blueberries

Directions

In a bowl, combine the flour, baking soda and salt. In a large mixing bowl, cream the shortening and sugar. Add eggs and vanilla; mix well. Beat in bananas. Gradually add the dry ingredients, beating just until combined. Fold in blueberries.

Pour into three greased 5-3/4-in. x 3-in. x 2-in. loaf pans. Bake at 350 degrees F for 30-35 minutes or until a toothpick inserted near the center comes out clean. Cool for 10 minutes before removing from pans to wire racks.

Cuban Banana Casserole

Ingredients

6 bananas, sliced lengthwise
1/2 cup light brown sugar
1/2 cup unsalted butter, cut into small pieces
1/2 cup chopped pecans
1/2 cup raisins
1 tablespoon brandy

Directions

Preheat oven to 350 degrees F (175 degrees C). Lightly butter a 9x13 inch casserole dish.

Cover the bottom of the prepared casserole dish with half of the banana slices. Sprinkle the bananas with half the brown sugar, butter pieces, pecans, and raisins. Form another layer with the remaining banana slices and repeat layering with remaining brown sugar, butter, pecans, and raisins.

Bake in preheated oven for 30 minutes; remove from oven and cool for 5 minutes. Sprinkle brandy over top of dish to serve.

Caribbean Banana Split

Ingredients

1 tablespoon unsalted butter
2 bananas, cut in half crosswise then lengthwise
1/4 cup dark rum
1/8 teaspoon ground nutmeg
1/8 teaspoon ground cinnamon
2 tablespoons lime juice
1 quart vanilla ice cream
1/4 cup chocolate syrup
1/2 cup whipped cream

Directions

Melt butter in a large nonstick skillet over medium-high heat. Cook bananas in butter until they are browned and begin to soften, about 1 minute. Remove pan from heat; stir in rum, nutmeg and cinnamon. Use a long match or lighter to carefully ignite the liquid in the pan. Allow to burn for 15 to 30 seconds; if necessary, extinguish by placing lid on pan.

Continue to cook until sauce has reduced by half, 2 to 3 minutes. Stir in lime juice; cook for 1 additional minute.

Divide ice cream between 4 serving bowls. Top each with the warm bananas and rum sauce mixture. Drizzle each sundae with chocolate sauce, and top with whipped cream.

Banana and Chocolate Bread Pudding

Ingredients

4 eggs
2 cups milk
1 cup SPLENDA® No Calorie
Sweetener, Granulated
1 tablespoon vanilla extract
4 cups cubed French bread
2 bananas, sliced
1 cup semisweet chocolate chips

Directions

Preheat oven to 350 degrees F (175 degrees C). Grease a 9x5 inch loaf pan.

In a large mixing bowl, mix eggs, milk, SPLENDA® Granulated Sweetener, and vanilla until smooth. Stir in bread, bananas, and chocolate chips, and let rest 5 minutes for bread to soak. Pour into prepared pan.

Line a roasting pan with a damp kitchen towel. Place loaf pan on towel inside roasting pan, and place roasting pan on oven rack. Fill roasting pan with water to reach halfway up the sides of the loaf pan. Bake in preheated oven for 1 hour, or until a knife inserted in the center comes out clean.

Banana Oatmeal Cookies II

Ingredients

3/4 cup shortening
1 cup packed brown sugar 1
egg
1/2 cup mashed ripe banana
1 teaspoon vanilla extract
1 cup all-purpose flour
1/2 teaspoon baking soda
1 teaspoon salt
1 teaspoon ground cinnamon
1/4 teaspoon ground cloves
3 cups rolled oats
1/2 cup chopped walnuts

Directions

Preheat oven to 350 degrees F (175 degrees C). Grease cookie sheets.

In a large bowl, cream together shortening and brown sugar. Beat in egg and mashed banana, then stir in vanilla. Combine flour, baking soda, salt, cinnamon, and cloves; stir into the banana mixture. Mix in rolled oats and walnuts. Drop by rounded spoonfuls onto prepared cookie sheets. Leave room for spreading.

Bake for 8 to 10 minutes in preheated oven. Allow cookies to cool on cookie sheets for 5 minutes before transferring to a wire rack to cool completely.

Moist Banana Muffins

Ingredients

2 cups flour
1 teaspoon baking soda
1 teaspoon baking powder
1 cup white sugar
3 ripe bananas, mashed
1 cup mayonnaise
1/2 cup chocolate chips (optional)

Directions

Preheat oven to 375 degrees F (190 degrees C). Grease 12 muffin cups or line with paper muffin liners.

Stir the flour, baking soda, baking powder, and sugar together in a bowl. Add the bananas, mayonnaise, and chocolate chips; stir until well combined. Pour into prepared muffin cups to about 3/4 full.

Bake in the preheated oven until golden and the tops spring back when lightly pressed, about 20 minutes.

Banana Nut and Ginger Bread

Ingredients

2 cups packed brown sugar
1 cup mashed bananas
2 eggs
1 teaspoon vanilla extract
2 tablespoons vegetable oil (optional)
3 cups all-purpose flour
2 teaspoons baking soda
1 teaspoon salt
1 1/2 teaspoons ground cinnamon
1/2 teaspoon ground allspice
1 tablespoon ground cardamom
1/2 teaspoon ground cloves
2 cups dark beer
1 1/2 cups chopped walnuts
2 tablespoons all-purpose flour
2 cups dates, pitted and chopped
2 tablespoons minced fresh ginger root

Directions

Preheat oven to 350 degrees F (175 degrees C). Lightly grease two 9x5 inch loaf pans.

In a large bowl cream the brown sugar, banana, eggs, and vanilla. For moister bread, add oil, if desired.

In a separate bowl, sift together 3 cups flour, baking soda, salt, cinnamon, all spice, cardamom, and cloves. Alternately blend the flour mixture and beer into the creamed mixture.

Toss the walnuts with the remaining flour. Stir in the dates and ginger to the mixture and blend well. Pour into two greased 9x5 loaf pans.

Bake in a 350 degree F (175 degrees C) oven for 1 hour, or until inserted toothpick emerges dry and clean.

Pisang Goreng (Indonesian Banana Fritters)

Ingredients

1 1/4 cups all-purpose flour
2 tablespoons granulated sugar
1/4 tablespoon vanilla powder
1/2 cup milk
1 egg
2 tablespoons butter, melted
1 teaspoon rum flavoring
4 ripe bananas, sliced
2 cups oil for frying

Directions

In a large bowl, combine flour, sugar and vanilla powder. Make a well in the center, and pour in milk, egg, melted butter and rum flavoring. Mix until smooth. Fold in banana slices until evenly coated.

Heat oil in a wok or deep-fryer to 375 degrees F (190 degrees C).

Drop banana mixture by tablespoon into hot oil. Fry until golden brown and crispy, 10 to 15 minutes. Remove bananas from oil, and drain on paper towels. Serve hot.

Chocolate-Banana Cake Roll

Ingredients

5 tablespoons unsweetened cocoa powder
1/2 cup all-purpose flour
1 tablespoon baking powder
5 egg yolks
3/4 cup white sugar, divided
5 egg whites
1 teaspoon vanilla extract
1 cup sweetened whipped cream
2 bananas, peeled
2 tablespoons confectioners' sugar for dusting
2 cups prepared chocolate frosting

Directions

Preheat the oven to 325 degrees F (165 degrees C). Line a 10x15 inch jellyroll pan with parchment paper. Sift together the cocoa, flour and baking powder; set aside.

In a medium bowl, whip the egg yolks and half of the sugar with an electric mixer until thick and pale. Set aside. In a separate larger bowl, combine the egg whites and vanilla. Whip with clean beaters until foamy. Gradually sprinkle in the remaining sugar while continuing to whip until stiff but not blocky. Fold the yolks into the whites by hand, then fold in the dry ingredients. Spread evenly in the prepared pan.

Bake for 15 minutes in the preheated oven, until the cake springs back when lightly pressed. Try not to let it bake too long or it will be difficult to roll. When the cake is done, run a knife around the edge to loosen and turn out onto a sheet of parchment paper or aluminum foil. Sprinkle confectioners' sugar on both sides and allow to cool.

Spread whipped cream on one side and place the bananas along the length. Roll the cake up around the bananas. Place on a serving platter with the seam side down. Frost with chocolate frosting.

Banana Flip

Ingredients

1 banana
1 3/4 cups milk
3 tablespoons powdered chocolate drink mix
2 tablespoons white sugar

Directions

In a blender, combine banana, milk, chocolate drink mix and sugar. Blend until smooth. Pour into glasses and serve.

Slow Cooker Bananas Foster

Ingredients

4 bananas, peeled and sliced
4 tablespoons butter, melted
1 cup packed brown sugar
1/4 cup rum
1 teaspoon vanilla extract 1/2
teaspoon ground cinnamon 1/4
cup chopped walnuts 1/4 cup
shredded coconut

Directions

Layer sliced bananas in the bottom of a slow cooker.

Combine butter, brown sugar, rum, vanilla and cinnamon in a small bowl; pour over bananas.

Cover and cook on Low for 2 hours. Top bananas with walnuts and coconut during the last 30 minutes of cooking.

Roasted Pecan Banana Bread Loaves

Ingredients

3/4 cup chopped pecans
1 1/2 cups all-purpose flour
1 teaspoon baking soda
1 teaspoon baking powder
1/4 teaspoon salt
1 1/2 cups very ripe, mashed bananas
1 cup white sugar
2 large eggs
1 1/2 teaspoons vanilla extract
1/2 teaspoon coconut extract
2 tablespoons lemon juice
1/2 cup light butter, at room temperature

Directions

Preheat oven to 275 degrees F (135 degrees C). Spread the pecans onto a baking sheet, and toast until the nuts start to turn golden brown and become fragrant, about 45 minutes. Watch the nuts carefully as they bake, they burn quickly. Once toasted, set the nuts aside to cool to room temperature.

Raise the oven temperature to 350 degrees F (175 degrees C). Spray 2 mini loaf pans with cooking spray.

Combine the toasted pecans, flour, baking soda, baking powder, and salt in a bowl. In a large bowl, mix the bananas, sugar, eggs, vanilla and coconut extracts, lemon juice, and butter together with a fork or an electric mixer on low speed. Stir the flour mixture into the banana mixture, and pour the batter into the prepared loaf pans, filling them about 3/4 full.

Bake in the preheated oven until a toothpick inserted into the middle of a loaf comes out clean, about 30 minutes. Let the loaves cool in the pans for 5 minutes before turning out onto a rack to finish cooling. Wrap cooled loaves in plastic wrap.

Banana Bran Zucchini Bread

Ingredients

1/4 cup canned pumpkin
1 very ripe banana, mashed
1 egg
2 egg whites
1 cup maple syrup
1/3 cup raw sugar, such as turbinado or demerara
1 tablespoon vanilla extract
2 cups grated unpeeled zucchini
2 cups whole wheat pastry flour
1 cup unprocessed bran
1 teaspoon salt
1 teaspoon baking soda
1/4 teaspoon baking powder
1 tablespoon ground cinnamon
1/2 teaspoon ground nutmeg 1/4 teaspoon ground cloves
1/4 teaspoon ground ginger
1/4 teaspoon ground allspice

Directions

Preheat oven to 350 degrees F (175 degrees C). Grease one 9x13 inch baking pan.

Stir together the pumpkin, banana, egg, and egg whites in a large bowl. Beat in maple syrup, sugar, and vanilla; the batter should be a bit frothy. Stir in zucchini; set aside.

Mix flour, bran, salt, baking soda, baking powder, cinnamon, nutmeg, cloves, ginger, and allspice in a separate bowl. Gradually add the flour mixture to the zucchini mixture, stirring just to moisten all ingredients. Over-mixing the batter will make it tough.

Pour the batter into the prepared pan. Bake until a toothpick inserted in the center comes out clean, 50 to 60 minutes. Cool completely before cutting into squares.

Easy Banana Pudding Parfaits

Ingredients

12 NILLA Wafers, divided
1/4 cup thawed COOL WHIP
Whipped Topping, divided
1 small banana, sliced, divided
2 JELL-O Vanilla Pudding Snacks

Directions

Crush 10 wafers to form coarse crumbs; place 1/4 crumbs in each of 2 parfait glasses. Top each with 1 Tbsp. COOL WHIP, 2 banana slices and half of 1 pudding snack. Repeat layers of crumbs, bananas and pudding.

Refrigerate 15 min. Meanwhile, wrap reserved banana slices tightly in plastic wrap; refrigerate until ready to use.

Top parfaits with remaining COOL WHIP, wafers and banana slices just before serving.

Banana Cream Cheesecake

Ingredients

Crust:
1 1/4 cups vanilla wafer crumbs
1/2 cup ground walnuts
5 tablespoons butter, melted

Filling:
4 (8 ounce) packages cream cheese, room temperature
1 1/8 cups white sugar
3 tablespoons all-purpose flour
4 eggs
1 cup sour cream
2 ripe bananas, mashed
1/4 cup banana liqueur
1 1/2 teaspoons vanilla extract

Topping:
1 1/2 teaspoons unflavored gelatin
3 tablespoons cold water
1 cup milk
1/3 cup white sugar
4 egg yolks
2 teaspoons vanilla extract
1 1/2 cups heavy cream, chilled
12 vanilla wafer cookies

Directions

Preheat the oven to 350 degrees F (175 degrees C). Grease the sides of a 9 inch springform pan. In a medium bowl, mix together the vanilla wafer crumbs, ground walnuts, and melted butter. Press into the bottom of the prepared pan.

In a large bowl, stir cream cheese to soften. Mix together 1 1/8 cup sugar and flour; stir into the cream cheese until smooth. Stir in eggs, one at a time, mixing until well blended after each one. Stir in sour cream, mashed banana, banana liqueur, and 1 1/2 teaspoons of vanilla. Pour over the crust in the springform pan.

Cover the bottom of the outside of the cheesecake pan with aluminum foil to prevent water from the water bath from seeping in. Place springform pan inside a larger pan. Place the whole thing into the preheated oven, and fill the outer pan with hot water.

Bake for 45 minutes in the preheated oven. After the time is up, turn the oven off, but leave door closed. Leave cheesecake in the unopened oven for 1 hour. Before removing from the water bath. Run a knife around the outer edge of the cake to keep it from shrinking away from the center and cracking. Let cool to room temperature, then refrigerate until chilled, at least 3 hours, or overnight.

In a small bowl, sprinkle the unflavored gelatin over the cold water, and set aside to soften. Heat milk in a small saucepan over medium-low heat until hot but not boiling. Meanwhile, whisk together 1/3 cup sugar and egg yolks until smooth and frothy. Whisk about 1/3 of the hot milk into the egg yolk mixture, then pour the yolk mixture into the pan with the remaining milk. Cook over low heat, stirring constantly with a spatula, making sure that the mixture does not burn on the bottom, until it is thick enough to coat the back of a metal spoon. Remove from the heat. Stir the softened gelatin into the hot pastry cream until dissolved, then stir in vanilla. Pour into a bowl, place a sheet of plastic wrap directly on the surface, and refrigerate until cooled, about 1 hour.

When the pastry cream is cooled, whip heavy cream just past soft peaks. Stir pastry cream to soften, then fold in the whipped cream. Place vanilla wafers on top of the cooled cheesecake, then spread the vanilla cream over the entire top. Chill until serving. Run a wet knife around the outer edge of the cake before removing the sides for a cleaner look.

Bailey's Banana Colada

Ingredients

2 bananas, broken into chunks
6 fluid ounces banana liqueur
6 fluid ounces Irish cream liqueur
6 fluid ounces coconut cream
6 cups crushed ice

Directions

In a blender combine the bananas and banana liqueur; blend until smooth. Blend in the Irish cream and coconut cream (Note: Make sure the coconut cream is at room temperature, or you will not be able to pour it). Finally, add the ice and blend until smooth.

Banana Macadamia Nut Bread

Ingredients

2/3 cup warm water (110 degrees F/45 degrees C)
3/4 cup mashed bananas
2 tablespoons margarine, softened
1 egg
3 1/4 cups bread flour
3 tablespoons white sugar
1 1/4 teaspoons salt
2 3/4 teaspoons active dry yeast
1/2 cup chopped macadamia nuts

Directions

Place ingredient in bread machine in order suggested by your manufacturer. Select sweet bread setting and light crust. Add macadamia nuts when indicated by your manufacturer.

Peanut Banana Waldorf

Ingredients

1 small unpeeled red apple, cored and cut into bite-size pieces
1 small firm banana, halved lengthwise and sliced
2 tablespoons peanuts
2 tablespoons mayonnaise
1 tablespoon peanut butter

Directions

In a bowl, combine the apple, banana and peanuts. Combine the mayonnaise and peanut butter; add to the fruit mixture and toss to coat. Serve immediately.

Dirty Banana

Ingredients

1 scoop vanilla ice cream
1 fluid ounce coffee flavored liqueur
1 fluid ounce banana liqueur
1/4 cup pineapple juice
1 tablespoon chocolate syrup
1/4 cup whipped cream
1 banana, sliced

Directions

In a blender, combine ice cream, coffee liqueur, banana liqueur and pineapple juice. Blend until smooth. Drizzle chocolate syrup decoratively into a fluted glass. Pour blended mixture into glasses and garnish with whipped cream and a slice of banana.

Banana Caramel Pie I

Ingredients

1 (14 ounce) can sweetened condensed milk
3 ripe bananas
1 (9 inch) prepared graham cracker crust
1 cup whipping cream
1/4 cup confectioners' sugar
2 (1.4 ounce) bars English toffee-flavored candy, crushed

Directions

Preheat oven to 350 degrees F (175 degrees C).

Pour the condensed milk into a small baking dish, and cover with aluminum foil. Place the dish in a larger baking pan. Pour boiling water into the larger pan so it surrounds the smaller dish and comes half way up the sides. Place in preheated oven. Bake 1 hour, stirring twice, until milk turns light brown, thick, and caramelized.

Slice the bananas and arrange on bottom of the graham cracker crust. Pour caramelized milk over bananas, and cool 30 minutes in the refrigerator.

Place the heavy cream in a medium bowl, and whip until soft peaks form. Gradually add the confectioners' sugar; and continue whipping until stiff peaks form. Spread whipped cream over cooled caramel. Sprinkle with crushed toffee. Chill 3 hours before serving.

Gramma Bertha's Banana Cake

Ingredients

1/2 cup butter
1 1/2 cups white sugar
4 eggs
3 bananas, sliced
1 cup sour cream
1 teaspoon baking soda
2 cups all-purpose flour

Directions

Preheat oven to 350 degrees F (175 degrees C). Spray a 10 inch Bundt pan with non-stick cooking spray.

In a large bowl, cream together the butter and sugar until light and fluffy. Beat in the eggs one at a time. Beat in the sliced bananas, sour cream and baking soda. Beat in the flour. Pour batter into prepared pan.

Bake in the preheated oven for 60 minutes, or until a toothpick inserted into the center of the cake comes out clean. Let cool in pan for 10 minutes, then turn out onto a wire rack and cool completely.

Banana Cream Supreme

Ingredients

2 cups graham cracker crumbs
1/2 cup melted butter
1/4 cup white sugar
1 (12 ounce) container frozen whipped topping, thawed
1 (3.5 ounce) package instant vanilla pudding mix
1 cup sour cream
3 bananas, sliced

Directions

In a medium bowl, combine crackers, butter and sugar. Press mixture into bottom and sides of a 9x13 inch pan.

In a large bowl, combine whipped topping, pudding and sour cream; whisk together. Put half of this mixture into crust. Layer sliced bananas over top of pie. Pour second half of pudding mixture over top of bananas.

Immediately cover and refrigerate pie for one hour.

Banana Bonkers

Ingredients

3 bananas
3 cups fresh grapefruit juice
2 cups lemon sherbet
1 cup crushed ice

Directions

Puree bananas in a blender or food processor. In a gallon pitcher combine pureed bananas, grapefruit juice, lemon sherbet and crushed ice. Stir and serve.

Bananasicles

Ingredients

4 medium bananas, peeled and halved horizontally
2 1/2 cups KELLOGG'S® RICE KRISPIES® cereal
1/2 cup coarsely chopped dried fruits or flaked coconut
1 (16 ounce) package vanilla-flavored candy coating or vanilla-almond bark
8 ice cream sticks

Directions

Place banana pieces on foil-lined baking sheet. Cover with plastic wrap. Freeze until needed.

In shallow dish combine KELLOGG'S® RICE KRISPIES® cereal and fruit. Set aside.

With adult help, in small saucepan melt candy coating according to package directions. Remove from heat. Pour into another shallow dish.

Remove bananas from freezer and insert an ice-cream stick into cut end of each banana piece. Dip banana halves into melted candy coating, letting excess drip off. Roll in cereal mixture until evenly coated. Return to baking sheet. Freeze for 15 minutes. Transfer to airtight container. Freeze for 2 hours to 1 week. Let stand at room temperature for 10 minutes before serving.

Grandma's Banana Bread

Ingredients

3 cups sugar
1 cup margarine, softened
1 teaspoon vanilla extract
4 eggs
3 1/2 cups all-purpose flour
2 teaspoons baking soda
1/4 teaspoon salt
1 cup buttermilk
6 very ripe bananas, mashed

Directions

Preheat oven to 325 degrees F (165 degrees C). Lightly grease a 9x13 inch baking pan.

In a large bowl, cream together the sugar and margarine until light and fluffy. Stir in the eggs one at a time, beating well with each addition, then stir in the vanilla.

In a large bowl, sift together flour, baking soda and salt. Blend this mixture into the egg mixture, alternately with the buttermilk; stir just to combine. Fold in the mashed bananas; mixing just enough to evenly combine. Pour batter into prepared pan.

Bake in preheated oven until a toothpick inserted into center of the loaf comes our clean, about 60 minutes.

Apple Banana Smoothie

Ingredients

1 frozen bananas, peeled and chopped
1/2 cup orange juice
1 Gala apple, peeled, cored and chopped
1/4 cup milk

Directions

In a blender combine frozen banana, orange juice, apple and milk. Blend until smooth. pour into glasses and serve.

Banana Loaf Cake II

Ingredients

1 (18.25 ounce) package yellow cake mix
1 (3.5 ounce) package instant banana pudding mix
1/2 cup mashed banana
4 eggs
1 cup water
1/4 cup vegetable oil
1/2 cup chopped walnuts

Directions

Preheat oven to 350 degrees F (175 degrees C). Grease and flour two 8x4 inch loaf pans.

In a medium bowl, stir together the cake mix and instant pudding. Add the eggs, oil, water and mashed banana, mix with an electric mixer until smooth. Fold in the chopped nuts. Pour evenly into the prepared pans.

Bake for 50 to 55 minutes in the preheated oven, until a toothpick inserted comes out clean. Cool in pans for 15 minutes before removing to cool completely on wire racks.

Lower Fat Banana Bread II

Ingredients

2 eggs
2/3 cup white sugar
2 very ripe bananas, mashed
1/4 cup applesauce
1/3 cup nonfat milk
1 tablespoon vegetable oil
1 tablespoon vanilla extract
1 3/4 cups all-purpose flour
2 teaspoons baking powder
1/2 teaspoon baking soda
1/2 teaspoon salt
1/3 cup chopped walnuts

Directions

Preheat oven to 325 degrees F (165 degrees C). Spray a bread pan with non-stick cooking spray, and lightly dust with flour.

In a large bowl, beat eggs and sugar in a large bowl until light and fluffy, about 5 minutes. Beat in bananas, applesauce, milk, oil and vanilla.

In a separate bowl, sift together flour, baking powder, baking soda and salt. Stir flour mixture into banana mixture, mixing just until blended. Fold in walnuts. Pour batter into prepared pan.

Bake in preheated pan until golden and a toothpick inserted into center of the loaf comes out clean, about 1 hour. Turn bread out onto a wire rack and let cool.

Chocolate Chip Banana Muffins

Ingredients

1 3/4 cups all-purpose flour
3/4 cup sugar
1 teaspoon baking powder
1 teaspoon baking soda
1/2 teaspoon salt
1 egg
1/2 cup vegetable oil
1/2 cup plain yogurt
1 teaspoon vanilla extract
1 cup mashed ripe bananas
3/4 cup semisweet chocolate chips

Directions

In a large bowl, combine the flour, sugar, baking powder, baking soda and salt. In another bowl, combine the egg, oil, yogurt and vanilla. Stir into dry ingredients just until moistened. Fold in bananas and chocolate chips. Fill greased or paper-lined muffin cups two-thirds full. Bake at 350 degrees F for 22-25 minutes or until a toothpick comes out clean. Cool for 5 minutes before removing from pans to wire racks.

Sole with Bananas

Ingredients

2 tablespoons butter
1 tablespoon all-purpose flour
1 cup milk
6 (4 ounce) fillets sole
1/2 cup white wine
2 tablespoons fresh lime juice
salt and pepper to taste
3 bananas, sliced lengthwise
1/4 cup grated Parmesan cheese

Directions

Preheat oven to 350 degrees F (175 degrees C).

In a medium saucepan over medium heat, blend the butter, flour, and milk. Cook, stirring constantly, until a thick sauce has formed.

Arrange sole in a single layer in a medium baking dish, and cover with the wine and lime juice. Season with salt and pepper. Pour 1/2 the sauce over the fish. Arrange bananas over the fish, and cover with remaining sauce. Sprinkle with Parmesan cheese.

Bake 25 minutes in the preheated oven, until the cheese is lightly browned and the fish is easily flaked with a fork. Drain any of the remaining wine and lime juice mixture before serving.

Banana Split Bars

Ingredients

2 cups all-purpose flour
1 cup white sugar
3/4 teaspoon baking soda
1/2 teaspoon salt
1/2 teaspoon ground cinnamon
1 (8 ounce) can crushed pineapple, with juice
2 eggs
1/2 cup vegetable oil
2 very ripe bananas, mashed
1 teaspoon vanilla extract
1/4 cup maraschino cherries, halved

1/4 cup butter, melted
1 teaspoon vanilla extract
3 cups confectioners' sugar
4 tablespoons milk

Directions

Preheat oven to 350 degrees F (175 degrees C). Grease and flour a 9x13 inch pan.

In a large bowl, mix together the flour, sugar, baking soda, salt and cinnamon. Make a well in the center and pour in the crushed pineapple, eggs, oil, bananas and 1 teaspoon vanilla. Stir in the cherries. Mix well and pour into prepared pan.

Bake in the preheated oven for 30 to 35 minutes, or until a toothpick inserted into the center of the cake comes out clean. Frost cake while still warm.

To make the frosting: in a medium bowl, combine melted butter, 1 teaspoon vanilla and confectioners' sugar. Beat in milk, one tablespoon at a time, until desired consistency is achieved.

Whole Grain Banana Muffins

Ingredients

3/4 cup whole wheat pastry flour
1/2 cup whole wheat flour
1 cup oat bran
1/4 cup sugar
1 tablespoon baking powder
1/2 teaspoon salt
3/4 cup raisins
1/2 cup nonfat plain yogurt
1/4 cup low fat sour cream
1/4 cup unsweetened applesauce
1/4 cup maple syrup
2 teaspoons egg whites
1 teaspoon vanilla extract
3 small ripe bananas, mashed
1/4 cup chopped pecans

Directions

Preheat oven to 400 degrees F (200 degrees C). Grease a 12 cup muffin tin.

In a large bowl, whisk together whole wheat flours, oat bran, sugar, baking powder, and salt. Stir in raisins. In another bowl, mix together yogurt, sour cream, applesauce, maple syrup, egg whites, vanilla, and bananas. Pour yogurt mixture into flour mixture, and mix just enough to combine. Spoon batter into muffin cups. Sprinkle one teaspoon pecans over batter in each cup.

Bake muffins in preheated oven for 15 to 20 minutes. Remove from oven, and transfer muffins to a wire rack to cool.

Banana Cake Cookies

Ingredients

1/2 cup shortening
1 cup packed brown sugar
2 eggs
1 cup mashed bananas
2 cups all-purpose flour
2 teaspoons baking powder
1/2 teaspoon baking soda
1/2 teaspoon salt
1/2 teaspoon ground cloves
1/2 cup chopped pecans
3 cups sifted confectioners' sugar
1 tablespoon butter, melted
3/4 teaspoon vanilla extract
3 tablespoons milk

Directions

Preheat oven to 350 degrees F (180 degrees C).

Cream shortening; add brown sugar, beating well. Add eggs and banana; beat well.

Sift together flour, baking powder, baking soda, salt, and spices. Add to creamed mixture; mix well. Stir in pecans.

Drop dough by rounded tablespoonfuls, 2 inches apart onto greased cookies sheets. Bake for 12 minutes. Remove to wire racks to cool. Dip half of cooled cookies into Powdered Sugar Icing.

To Make Icing: Combine 3 cups confectioner's sugar, 1 tablespoon melted butter or margarine, and 3/4 teaspoon vanilla extract. Add milk to yield desired consistency (you may need to add a little extra), beating until smooth.

Banana Blueberry Pie

Ingredients

1 (8 ounce) package cream cheese, softened
3/4 cup sugar
2 cups whipped topping
4 medium firm bananas, sliced
2 (9 inch) pastry shells, baked
1 (21 ounce) can blueberry pie filling
fresh blueberries and mint and additional sliced bananas (optional)

Directions

In a mixing bowl, beat cream cheese and sugar until smooth. Fold in whipped topping and bananas. Pour into pastry shells. Spread with pie filling. Refrigerate for at least 30 minutes. Just before serving, garnish with blueberries, mint and bananas if desired.

Banana Bread I

Ingredients

1 1/2 cups all-purpose flour
1 teaspoon baking soda
1/2 teaspoon salt
1 cup white sugar
2 eggs, beaten
1/4 cup butter, melted
3 bananas, mashed

Directions

Grease and flour two 7x3 inch loaf pans. Preheat oven to 350 degrees F (175 degrees C).

In one bowl, whisk together flour, soda, salt, and sugar. Mix in slightly beaten eggs, melted butter, and mashed bananas. Stir in nuts if desired. Pour into prepared pans.

Bake at 350 degrees F (175 degrees C) for 1 hour, or until a wooden toothpick inserted in the center comes out clean.

Banana Bread - Quick Bread for Machines

Ingredients

2 cups all-purpose flour
1 teaspoon baking powder
1/2 teaspoon baking soda
3/4 cup white sugar
3 tablespoons vegetable oil
2 eggs
2 bananas, peeled and halved lengthwise

Directions

Place ingredients in the pan of the bread machine.

Select the Dough setting, and press Start. Mix the bread for 3 to 5 minutes until the bananas are mashed and all ingredients are thoroughly combined. If necessary, use a rubber spatula to push the dough from the sides of the bread pan. When 3 to 5 minutes have passed on the clock display, press Stop. Do not continue mixing. Smooth out the top of the loaf with the rubber spatula.

Select the Bake setting, and press Start. The Bake cycle time may vary with machines, but should be about 50 minutes. To test the bread for doneness, insert a toothpick into the center top. Remove the toothpick. If the bread is done, the toothpick will come out clean. If there is dough on the toothpick, reset the machine on Bake and continue to bake an additional 10 to 15 minutes. Test again with the toothpick to assure the bread is completely baked. Remove the pan from the machine, but allow the bread to remain in the pan for 10 minutes. Remove the bread to cool completely on a wire rack.

Banana Coconut Loaf

Ingredients

2 eggs
1 cup white sugar
1/2 cup butter, melted
1 cup mashed bananas
1/2 teaspoon almond extract
1 1/2 cups all-purpose flour
1/2 cup flaked coconut
1 1/2 teaspoons baking powder
1/2 teaspoon baking soda
1/2 teaspoon salt
1/2 cup chopped walnuts
1/2 cup maraschino cherries, chopped

Directions

Mix together flour, coconut, baking powder, baking soda, salt, chopped walnuts, and cherries.

Break eggs in a mixing bowl, and beat until light and frothy. Add sugar and melted butter or margarine. Beat well. Stir in mashed banana and flavoring. Add flour mixture, and stir just to combine. Spoon into greased 9x5x3 inch loaf pan.

Bake at 350 degrees F (175 degrees C) for 1 hour, or until a toothpick inserted in center comes out clean. Let stand for 10 minutes, and remove from pan. Cool.

Bacon Fried Bananas

Ingredients

1 pound bacon
3 ripe bananas, sliced

Directions

Place the bacon in a large, deep skillet; cook over medium-high heat, turning occasionally, until evenly browned, about 10 minutes. Drain the bacon slices on a paper towel-lined plate.

Reduce heat to medium. Place the bananas cut side down and cook one minute. Flip with a spatula and cook an additional minute. Drain the banana slices on a paper towel-lined plate. Serve warm with bacon.

Banana Pumpkin Bread

Ingredients

2 ripe bananas, mashed
2 eggs
1/3 cup vegetable oil
1 1/3 cups canned pumpkin puree
1/2 cup honey
1/2 cup white sugar
2 1/2 cups all-purpose flour
1 teaspoon baking powder
1 teaspoon baking soda
1/2 teaspoon salt
2 teaspoons pumpkin pie spice
1 teaspoon ground cinnamon
3/4 cup raisins (optional)

Directions

Preheat oven to 350 degrees F (175 degrees C). Grease an 9x5 inch loaf pan.

In a large bowl, stir together the mashed banana, eggs, oil, pumpkin, honey and sugar. Combine the flour, baking powder, baking soda, salt, pie spice and cinnamon, stir into the banana mixture until just combined. Fold in the raisins and walnuts if desired. Pour batter into the prepared pan.

Bake at 350 degrees F (175 degrees C) for 45 minutes, or until a toothpick inserted into the center of the loaf comes out clean. Cool loaf in the pan for 10 minutes before moving to a wire rack to cool completely.

Banana Chocolate Chip Softies

Ingredients

1 1/4 cups all-purpose flour
1 teaspoon baking powder
1/2 teaspoon salt
1/3 cup butter, softened
1/4 cup light brown sugar
1 ripe banana, mashed
1 egg
1 teaspoon vanilla extract
3/4 cup milk chocolate chips

Directions

Preheat oven to 350 degrees F (175 degrees C). Grease cookie sheets. Sift together the flour, baking powder and salt, set aside.

In a medium bowl, cream together the butter and brown sugar. Beat in the banana and egg, then stir in the vanilla. Gradually stir in the dry ingredients until well blended. Fold in the chocolate chips and walnuts, if desired. Drop by rounded spoonfuls onto the prepared cookie sheets.

Bake for 8 to 10 minutes in the preheated oven. Allow cookies to cool on baking sheet for 5 minutes before removing to a wire rack to cool completely.

Peanut Butter Banana Melties

Ingredients

4 large bananas
1/2 cup peanut butter
1/2 cup chocolate chips

Directions

Leaving the peel on the bananas, slice each in half lengthwise. Smear the inside with peanut butter, and sprinkle with chocolate chips. Place the two halves back together and wrap each banana individually in aluminum foil.

Cook in the hot coals of a campfire until the banana is hot, and the chocolate has melted, about 10 to 15 minutes, depending on the heat of the coals.

Raspberry Banana Tofu Shake

Ingredients

1 (12 ounce) package firm silken tofu
1 cup fat free soy milk
1 banana
1 cup raspberries
1/4 cup frozen orange juice concentrate

Directions

In a blender, mix tofu, soy milk, banana, raspberries, and orange juice concentrate. Blend until smooth.

Banana Leaf Seafood

Ingredients

6 shallots, finely chopped
4 cloves garlic, peeled and crushed
2 tablespoons sambal belachan
2 teaspoons vegetable oil
1 teaspoon curry powder
1 teaspoon ground cumin
1 teaspoon fresh lime juice
salt and pepper to taste
1 pound squid, cleaned and sliced into rings
1 banana leaf

Directions

In a medium, non-reactive bowl, mix shallots, garlic, sambal belachan, vegetable oil, curry powder, cumin, lime juice, salt, and pepper. Place squid in the mixture. Cover, and marinate in the refrigerator at least 2 hours.

Preheat an outdoor grill for high heat, and lightly oil grate.

Lightly grease the banana leaf. Wrap squid in the leaf, and place on the prepared grill. Cook 10 to 15 minutes, until leaf is slightly charred and squid is opaque.

Banana Walnut Cornbread

Ingredients

2 tablespoons honey
2 bananas, mashed
1/4 cup vegetable oil
1/2 cup milk
2 teaspoons vanilla extract
1 cup cornmeal
1 cup whole wheat pastry flour
1 tablespoon baking powder
1 teaspoon baking soda
1/2 teaspoon ground cinnamon
1 1/2 cups chopped walnuts
1 banana, sliced

Directions

Preheat oven to 350 degrees F (175 degrees C). Lightly grease a 8x8 inch baking pan.

Place the honey, mashed bananas, canola oil, milk and vanilla into a blender or food processor; puree until smooth.

Sift together cornmeal, whole wheat flour, baking powder, soda and cinnamon. Stir flour mixture into banana mixture until blended. Fold in walnuts and sliced bananas. Pour into prepared pan.

Bake in preheated oven for 40 to 50 minutes, or until brown on top.

Coconut Banana Chocolate Cream Pie

Ingredients

1 1/3 cups cold water
2/3 cup nonfat dry milk powder
1 (1.4 ounce) package sugar-free instant chocolate pudding mix
1 cup reduced-fat whipped topping, divided
1/2 teaspoon coconut extract, divided
2 medium ripe bananas, cut into 1/4-inch slices
1 chocolate crumb crust (9 inches)
1 tablespoon flaked coconut, toasted

Directions

In a bowl, stir water and milk powder until powder is dissolved. Add pudding mix; whisk for 1-2 minutes or until thickened. Fold in 1/4 cup whipped topping and 1/4 teaspoon extract. Layer banana slices in the crust; top with pudding mixture. Cover and refrigerate.

Combine remaining whipped topping and extract; spread over pudding. Sprinkle with coconut. Cover and refrigerate for at least 1hour before serving.

Banana Cream Pie Made Easy

Ingredients

3 cups heavy cream
1/2 cup crushed ice
1 (3.5 ounce) package instant banana pudding mix
1 (3.4 ounce) package instant vanilla pudding mix
3 bananas, sliced
1 (9 inch) pie shell, baked

1 cup heavy cream

Directions

Using an electric mixer, whip 3 cups heavy cream on low speed until it starts to thicken. Add crushed ice and continue to whip another 4 minutes. Increase speed and add vanilla and banana pudding mixes, whipping until pudding mixes are blended fully with the cream and the mixture thickens. Increase speed to high and beat until mixture is stiff.

Line the bottom and half way up the sides of pie crust with banana slices. Cover bananas with half of the banana cream mixture and top completely with banana slices. Top with the remaining banana cream mixture.

In a small bowl, whip 1 cup cream until stiff peaks form. Using a pastry bag, pipe cream onto top of pie, covering completely. Refrigerate 1 hour before serving.

Caribbean Banana Muffins

Ingredients

2 cups all-purpose flour
1 teaspoon baking soda 1/2
teaspoon baking powder 1/2
teaspoon salt
1/2 cup butter
1 cup brown sugar
2 large eggs
3 medium bananas
1 tablespoon rum extract
1 cup shredded coconut
1/2 cup chopped dried pineapple

Directions

Preheat oven to 350 degrees F (175 degrees C). Prepare 12 muffin cups with paper liners.

Sift the flour, baking soda, baking powder, and salt into a bowl; set aside. In a large bowl, cream together butter and sugar until light and fluffy. Beat in the eggs one at a time, mixing well after each addition, then beat in the bananas and rum extract. Stir in the flour mixture. Fold in the shredded coconut and pineapple; mixing just enough to evenly distribute. Evenly divide the batter among the prepared muffin cups.

Bake in preheated oven until a toothpick inserted into the center comes out clean, 20 to 25 minutes.

White Chocolate Banana Pie

Ingredients

2 cups heavy whipping cream
6 (1 ounce) squares white chocolate
3 teaspoons vanilla extract
2 medium firm bananas. sliced
Lemon Juice
1 (9 inch) pastry shell, baked

Directions

In a saucepan, cook and stir the cream and chocolate over low heat until chocolate is melted. Remove from the heat; stir in vanilla. Transfer to a mixing bowl. Cover and refrigerate for 6 hours or until thickened, stirring occasionally.

Beat on high speed until light and fluffy, about 4 minutes (do not overbeat). Dip banana slices in lemon juice. Pour half of the cream mixture into pastry shell. Top with bananas. Cover with remaining cream mixture. Refrigerate until serving.

Banana Chocolate Chip Muffins

Ingredients

2 cups all-purpose flour
1/3 cup white sugar
2 tablespoons Dutch process cocoa powder
1 tablespoon baking powder
1 cup mashed bananas
2/3 cup canola oil
1 egg, beaten
1 cup semi-sweet chocolate chips

Directions

In a large bowl combine the flour, sugar, cocoa powder and baking powder.

In another bowl, blend the bananas, oil and egg together. Add to dry ingredients, mixing just until blended. Fold in the chocolate chips. Spoon the batter into a greased muffin pan, filling three-fourths full.

Bake in a preheated 425 degree F(220 degrees C) for 15 to 20 minutes. Remove the muffins to a wire rack to cool completely.

Almost No Fat Banana Bread

Ingredients

1 1/2 cups all-purpose flour
3/4 cup white sugar
1 1/4 teaspoons baking powder
1/2 teaspoon baking soda
1/2 teaspoon ground cinnamon
2 egg whites
1 cup banana, mashed
1/4 cup applesauce

Directions

Preheat oven to 350 degrees F (175 degrees C). Lightly grease an 8x4 inch loaf pan.

In a large bowl, stir together flour, sugar, baking powder, baking soda and cinnamon. Add egg whites, bananas and applesauce; stir just until combined. Pour batter into prepared pan.

Bake in preheated oven for 50 to 55 minutes, until a toothpick inserted into center of loaf comes out clean. Turn out onto wire rack and allow to cool before slicing.

Banana Spice Cookies

Ingredients

1/2 cup butter
2 1/4 cups all-purpose flour
1 cup white sugar
2 eggs
1 teaspoon vanilla extract
1/2 teaspoon ground cinnamon
1/4 teaspoon baking soda
1/8 teaspoon ground cloves
3 ripe bananas, mashed
1 teaspoon baking powder
1/2 cup chopped walnuts

Directions

Preheat oven to 375 degrees F (190 degrees C).

Beat butter or margarine with an electric mixer on medium to high speed for 30 seconds. Add one cup of the flour, the sugar, eggs, baking powder, vanilla, cinnamon, soda, and cloves. Beat until thoroughly combined.

Stir in the remaining flour. Beat in bananas and nuts. Drop by rounded teaspoons 2 inches apart onto a greased cookie sheet. Bake for 8 to 10 minutes or until edges are lightly browned. Cool cookies on a rack.

Banana Yogurt Pie

Ingredients

2 cups rolled oats
1 cup pitted dates
1 teaspoon vanilla extract
2 tablespoons orange juice
3 tablespoons cocoa powder
1/4 cup boiling water
1 teaspoon unflavored gelatin
2 frozen bananas, peeled and chopped
1 cup low-fat evaporated milk, chilled
1/2 teaspoon vanilla extract
1 cup low-fat plain yogurt
1 banana, finely sliced
1/4 cup lemon juice
1 teaspoon ground nutmeg

Directions

Combine the rolled oats, dates, vanilla extract, orange juice, and cocoa powder in the bowl of a food processor. Blend for 3 minutes, or until mixture sticks together. Press the mixture thinly around the sides and base of a 9 inch pie dish and refrigerate.

Place the gelatin in a small bowl. Pour boiling water over gelatin, stir to dissolve, and set aside to cool.

Place frozen bananas in food processor or blender and blend until smooth. Add milk and blend for 3-4 minutes. Add extra vanilla and yogurt and mix well. Add dissolved gelatin. Pour mixture into the base of the pie dish and refrigerate until firm.

Soak the extra banana in the lemon juice, slice and place on top of pie. Sprinkle with nutmeg and serve.

Banana Split Cream Puffs

Ingredients

1 cup water
1/2 cup butter or margarine
1 cup all-purpose flour
1/4 teaspoon salt
4 eggs
12 scoops vanilla ice cream
1 cup sliced fresh strawberries
1 large banana, thinly sliced
1 (8 ounce) can pineapple tidbits, drained
1/2 cup hot fudge sauce

Directions

In a saucepan over medium heat, bring water and butter to a boil. Add flour and salt all at once; stir until a smooth ball forms. Remove from the heat; let stand 5 minutes. Add eggs, one at a time, beating well after each addition. Beat until mixture is smooth and shiny, about 3 minutes. Drop by rounded tablespoonfuls onto a greased baking sheet. Bake at 400 degrees F for 30 to 35 minutes or until golden brown. Transfer to a wire rack. Immediately split puffs open; remove tops and set aside. Discard soft dough from inside. Cool puffs. Fill each with a scoop of ice cream and top with fruit. Drizzle with hot fudge sauce. Replace tops and serve immediately.

The Best Banana Bread

Ingredients

1/2 cup margarine, softened
1 cup white sugar
2 eggs
1 1/2 cups mashed banana
2 cups all-purpose flour
1 teaspoon baking soda

Directions

Preheat oven to 350 degrees F (175 degrees C). Grease and flour one 9x5 inch pan.

Cream margarine and sugar until smooth. Beat in eggs, then bananas. Add flour and soda, stirring just until combined.

Pour into prepared pan and bake at 350 degrees F (175 degrees C) for about 1 hour (or till toothpick comes out clean). Remove from pan and let cool, store in refrigerator or freeze.

Banana Split Freeze

Ingredients

3/4 cup SPLENDA® No Calorie Sweetener, Granulated
8 ounces cream cheese, softened
1 (20 ounce) can crushed pineapple, drained
1 (10 ounce) package frozen strawberries, thawed
2 bananas, diced
1 (8 ounce) tub frozen whipped topping, thawed

Directions

In a medium bowl, cream together SPLENDA® Granulated Sweetener and cream cheese until smooth. In a separate bowl, mix together the pineapple, strawberries, bananas, and whipped topping. Fold the fruit mixture into the cream cheese mixture until evenly blended.

Spread into a 9x13 inch glass dish, or divide among several smaller serving dishes. Cover with plastic wrap, and freeze overnight.

Thaw for approximately 20 minutes before serving.

Lowfat Chocolate Banana Parfaits

Ingredients

2 cups cold fat free milk
1 pkg. (4 serving size) JELL-O
Chocolate Flavor Fat Free Sugar
Free Instant Reduced Calorie
Pudding and Pie Filling
2 medium bananas, sliced
3/4 cup thawed COOL WHIP LITE
Whipped Topping, divided

Directions

Pour milk into medium bowl. Add pudding mix. Beat with wire whisk 2 minutes or until well blended.

Spoon half of the pudding evenly into 4 dessert glasses. Cover with layers of banana slices, 1/2 cup of the whipped topping and remaining pudding. Top with remaining whipped topping.

Refrigerate until ready to serve.

Berry Banana Smoothies

Ingredients

1 1/2 cups vanilla or plain yogurt
2/3 cup orange juice
2 ripe bananas, cut into chunks
1 cup halved fresh strawberries
2 teaspoons honey

Directions

In a blender, combine all ingredients; cover and process until smooth. Pour into chilled glasses; serve immediately.

Banana Angel Food Cake

Ingredients

1 1/2 cups egg whites
1/2 teaspoon cream of tartar
1/4 teaspoon baking powder
1 teaspoon vanilla extract 1/2
teaspoon ground cinnamon 1/4
cup rolled oats
3 ripe bananas, mashed
1 cup cake flour
2 cups confectioners' sugar
1/4 teaspoon salt

Directions

Preheat oven to 325 degrees F (165 degrees C).

Beat egg whites until stiff but not dry.

Combine cream of tartar, baking powder, vanilla, cinnamon, oats, and mashed bananas.

In a separate bowl combine the flour, confectioner's sugar, and salt.

Fold the banana mixture into the egg whites. Then fold the flour mixture into the egg white/banana mixture. Pour batter into one 9 or 10 inch round cake pan, coated with a non-stick cooking spray.

Bake at 325 degrees (165 degrees C) for 1 hour, until cake is firm and lightly golden. Cool for five minutes then slip out of pan onto a serving dish. Garnish with a light dusting of confectioner's sugar.

Delicious Raisin Nut Banana Bread

Ingredients

2 cups raisin nut bran cereal
1/2 cup milk
1 1/2 cups all-purpose flour
3 1/2 teaspoons baking powder
1 teaspoon baking soda
1/4 teaspoon salt
1 cup mashed ripe banana
1/2 cup white sugar
1/4 cup brown sugar
1/4 cup vegetable oil
1 egg

Directions

Preheat oven to 350 degrees F (175 degrees C). Lightly grease the bottom of a 9x5 inch loaf pan.

In a bowl, combine the raisin nut bran cereal and milk; let stand for 5 minutes.

In a large bowl, sift together flour, baking powder, baking soda and salt. In a separate bowl, beat together mashed banana, sugar, brown sugar, vegetable oil and egg. Combine the cereal and banana mixtures. Stir in the flour mixture just until combined. Pour batter into prepared pan.

Bake in preheated oven for 50 to 55 minutes, until a toothpick inserted into center of loaf comes out clean. Let cool before slicing.

Banana Colada

Ingredients

2 ripe bananas, mashed
4 fluid ounces cream of coconut
6 fluid ounces rum
4 fluid ounces banana liqueur
3 cups crushed ice

Directions

In a blender, combine bananas, cream of coconut, rum, banana liqueur and ice. Blend until smooth. Pour into glasses and serve.

Banana Split Dessert

Ingredients

1 cup miniature marshmallows
1 (8 ounce) can crushed pineapple, drained
1 cup whipped topping
2 small firm bananas. split lengthwise
Chocolate syrup
2 maraschino cherries

Directions

In a bowl, combine the marshmallows, pineapple and whipped topping. Place banana halves in dessert dishes with two scoops of marshmallow mixture between. Drizzle with chocolate syrup; top with a cherry. Serve immediately.

Carla's Baked Bananas

Ingredients

1 tablespoon cornstarch
1/2 cup sugar
1 cup water
2 tablespoons butter
1 1/2 teaspoons lemon juice
1/8 teaspoon ground nutmeg
1 pinch salt (optional)
7 ripe bananas

Directions

Preheat oven to 350 degrees F (175 degrees C).

In a saucepan over medium-high heat, mix together cornstarch and sugar. Gradually stir in water. Bring to a boil, stirring constantly. Remove from heat, stir in butter, lemon juice, nutmeg, and salt.

Peel bananas, and place in a casserole dish. Drizzle sauce over bananas.

Bake in a preheated oven for 12 minutes. Serve warm.

Sour Cream Banana Cake

Ingredients

2 cups packed brown sugar
1 cup sour cream
1 cup butter
1 teaspoon baking soda
4 eggs
1/8 teaspoon salt
4 bananas
2 teaspoons vanilla extract
4 cups sifted cake flour
1 cup chopped walnuts
1/2 cup butter
4 cups confectioners' sugar
1/4 cup sour cream
1 teaspoon vanilla extract

Directions

Cream brown sugar and 1 cup butter, add eggs 1 at a time; beat well. Add mashed bananas and flour and salt, baking soda along with 1 cup sour cream . Add vanilla and nuts last.

Pour batter into 3 - 9 inch pans or a 13 x 9 inch pan. Bake in a preheated 350 degrees F (175 degrees C) oven until cake tests done with a tooth pick, about 30 to 40 minutes for the 9 inch round cakes or about 40 to 50 minutes for the 13 x 9 inch cake..

To make Frosting: Mix 1/2 cup of butter or margarine, 4 cups of confectioners' sugar and 1/4 cup sour cream (more if needed). Add 1 teaspoon vanilla and beat until fluffy.

Banana Muffins II

Ingredients

1 1/2 cups all-purpose flour
1 teaspoon baking powder
1 teaspoon baking soda
1/2 teaspoon salt
3 large bananas, mashed
3/4 cup white sugar
1 egg
1/3 cup butter, melted

Directions

Preheat oven to 350 degrees F (175 degrees C). Coat muffin pans with non-stick spray, or use paper liners. Sift together the flour, baking powder, baking soda, and salt; set aside.

Combine bananas, sugar, egg, and melted butter in a large bowl. Fold in flour mixture, and mix until smooth. Scoop into muffin pans.

Bake in preheated oven. Bake mini muffins for 10 to 15 minutes, and large muffins for 25 to 30 minutes. Muffins will spring back when lightly tapped.

Triple Layer Banana Cream Pie Bars

Ingredients

1 1/2 cups crushed NILLA Wafers
1/2 cup PLANTERS Chopped Pecans
1/3 cup butter or margarine, melted
3 bananas, sliced
3 cups cold milk
2 pkg. (4 serving size) JELL-O Vanilla Flavor Instant Pudding
2 1/2 cups thawed COOL WHIP Whipped Topping, divided

Directions

Preheat oven to 325 degrees F. Mix wafer crumbs, pecans and butter in 13x9-inch baking dish; press firmly onto bottom of dish. Bake 8 min. Cool 10 min.

Top crust with banana slices. Pour milk into large bowl. Add pudding mixes. Beat with wire whisk 2 min. or until well blended. Spoon 2 cups of the pudding over banana layer.

Gently stir 1 cup of the whipped topping into remaining pudding; spoon over pie. Top with remaining 1-1/2 cups whipped topping. Refrigerate 3 hours. Store any leftovers in refrigerator.

Banana-Dulce de Leche Pie (Banana-Caramel Pie)

Ingredients

1 (14 ounce) can sweetened condensed milk
1 cup graham cracker crumbs
1/2 cup butter, melted
4 bananas
1 1/2 cups whipping cream
2 tablespoons confectioners' sugar
1 teaspoon vanilla extract

Directions

To make dulce de leche, place the unopened can of sweetened condensed milk in a saucepan, and add enough water to cover half-way up the can. Place the saucepan over medium-high heat and bring to a boil. Cook for 3 hours, adding more water as necessary. Remove from heat and cool.

Preheat oven to 350 degrees F (175 degrees C).

Combine the graham cracker crumbs with the butter in a mixing bowl until evenly blended. Press the crumb mixture evenly into a 9 inch pie plate.

Bake pie crust in preheated oven until lightly browned, 10-15 minutes. Remove from oven, and cool on a wire rack.

Open the can of dulce de leche, and pour half, or about 3/4 cup, over the pie crust. Slice the bananas and arrange half in a layer over the dulce de leche filling. Pour the remaining dulce de leche over the bananas. Top with remaining banana slices.

Pour the whipping cream into a mixing bowl, and beat until soft peaks form. Add the sugar and vanilla extract; continue beating until stiff peaks form. Spoon the whipped cream over the bananas. Chill at least 1 hour before serving.

Banana Split Bread

Ingredients

2/3 cup shortening
1 1/4 cups sugar
4 eggs
3 1/2 cups all-purpose flour
2 1/2 teaspoons baking powder
1 teaspoon baking soda
1/2 teaspoon salt
1 1/2 cups mashed ripe bananas
2 (8 ounce) cans crushed pineapple, drained
2 cups semisweet chocolate chips
1 (10 ounce) jar maraschino cherries, drained and chopped
1 cup chopped walnuts

Directions

In a mixing bowl, cream shortening and sugar. Add eggs, one at a time, beating well after each addition. Combine the flour, baking powder, baking soda and salt; add to creamed mixture alternately with banana and pineapple. Fold in the chocolate chips, cherries and walnuts. Pour into two greased 9-in. x 5-in. x 3-in. loaf pans. Bake at 350 degrees F for 60-65 minutes or until a toothpick comes out clean. Cool for 10 minutes before removing from pans to wire racks.

Chocolate Banana Bread Pudding

Ingredients

4 eggs
2 cups milk
1 cup white sugar
1 tablespoon vanilla extract
4 cups cubed French bread
2 bananas, sliced
1 cup semisweet chocolate chips

Directions

Preheat oven to 350 degrees F (175 degrees C). Grease a 9x5 inch loaf pan.

In a large mixing bowl, mix eggs, milk, sugar, and vanilla until smooth. Stir in bread, bananas, and chocolate chips, and let rest 5 minutes for bread to soak. Pour into prepared pan.

Line a roasting pan with a damp kitchen towel. Place loaf pan on towel inside roasting pan, and place roasting pan on oven rack. Fill roasting pan with water to reach halfway up the sides of the loaf pan. Bake in preheated oven for 1 hour, or until a knife inserted in the center comes out clean.

The Greatest Banana Bread

Ingredients

1 3/4 cups all-purpose flour
1 cup white sugar
1 teaspoon baking soda
3 ripe bananas, mashed
2 eggs
1/2 cup vegetable oil
5 tablespoons buttermilk
1 teaspoon vanilla extract
1/2 cup chopped walnuts

Directions

Preheat oven to 325 degrees F (165 degrees C). Grease and flour an 8x4 inch loaf pan.

In a separate bowl mash bananas to equal 1 cup and add oil, eggs, buttermilk and vanilla extract. Beat together and pour this mixture into the dry ingredients. Add nuts and stir just until combined. Pour batter into 8x4 inch loaf pan.

Bake for 1 hour and 20 minutes in the preheated oven, or until a toothpick inserted into the cake comes out clean.

Banana Crumb Muffins

Ingredients

1 1/2 cups all-purpose flour
1 teaspoon baking soda
1 teaspoon baking powder
1/2 teaspoon salt
3 bananas, mashed
3/4 cup white sugar
1 egg, lightly beaten
1/3 cup butter, melted
1/3 cup packed brown sugar
2 tablespoons all-purpose flour
1/8 teaspoon ground cinnamon
1 tablespoon butter

Directions

Preheat oven to 375 degrees F (190 degrees C). Lightly grease 10 muffin cups, or line with muffin papers.

In a large bowl, mix together 1 1/2 cups flour, baking soda, baking powder and salt. In another bowl, beat together bananas, sugar, egg and melted butter. Stir the banana mixture into the flour mixture just until moistened. Spoon batter into prepared muffin cups.

In a small bowl, mix together brown sugar, 2 tablespoons flour and cinnamon. Cut in 1 tablespoon butter until mixture resembles coarse cornmeal. Sprinkle topping over muffins.

Bake in preheated oven for 18 to 20 minutes, until a toothpick inserted into center of a muffin comes out clean.

Southern Style Banana Split Cake

Ingredients

2 cups graham cracker crumbs
3/4 cup white sugar
1/4 pound butter, melted
2 (8 ounce) packages cream cheese
1 1/2 cups confectioners' sugar
4 bananas, sliced
1 (15 ounce) can crushed pineapple, drained
1 (16 ounce) container frozen whipped topping, thawed
1 (16 ounce) jar maraschino cherries, drained
12 ounces crushed peanuts

Directions

Combine the graham cracker crumbs, white sugar and melted butter. Mix together and press into a 9x13 inch cake pan; refrigerate until chilled.

Beat together the cream cheese and confectioners sugar; spread over graham cracker crust.

Layer bananas and pineapple over cream cheese mixture; cover fruit with whipped topping.

Top with cherries and chopped nuts; refrigerate and serve chilled.

Jemput Jumput (Banana Fritters)

Ingredients

5/8 cup all-purpose flour
1 pinch salt
1 teaspoon baking powder
6 ripe bananas
3 tablespoons white sugar
oil for frying

Directions

Heat oil in a deep fryer or heavy bottomed pan to 375 degrees F (190 degrees C).

Sift the flour, salt, and baking powder into a medium bowl.

In a separate bowl, mash together the bananas and sugar. Gradually mix flour mixture into mashed bananas, stirring until well combined.

Drop batter by spoonfuls into hot oil, and cook, turning once, until browned, 2 to 8 minutes. Drain on paper towels.

Lightning Source UK Ltd.
Milton Keynes UK
UKHW050750160621
385475UK00004B/238